Practical Highcharts with Angular

Your Essential Guide to Creating Real-time Dashboards

Second Edition

Sourabh Mishra

Apress®

Practical Highcharts with Angular:Your Essential Guide to Creating Real-time Dashboards

Sourabh Mishra
Bangalore, India

ISBN-13 (pbk): 978-1-4842-9180-1   ISBN-13 (electronic): 978-1-4842-9181-8
https://doi.org/10.1007/978-1-4842-9181-8

Managing Director, Apress Media LLC: Welmoed Spahr
Acquisitions Editor: Divya Modi
Development Editor:James Markham
Coordinating Editor: Divya Modi
Copy Editor: Mary Behr

Cover image designed by eStudioCalamar

Distributed to the book trade worldwide by Springer Science+Business Media New York, 1 New York Plaza, Suite 4600, New York, NY 10004-1562, USA. Phone 1-800-SPRINGER, fax (201) 348-4505, e-mail orders-ny@ springer-sbm.com, or visit www.springeronline.com. Apress Media, LLC is a California LLC and the sole member (owner) is Springer Science + Business Media Finance Inc (SSBM Finance Inc). SSBM Finance Inc is a **Delaware** corporation.

For information on translations, please e-mail booktranslations@springernature.com; for reprint, paperback, or audio rights, please e-mail bookpermissions@springernature.com.

Apress titles may be purchased in bulk for academic, corporate, or promotional use. eBook versions and licenses are also available for most titles. For more information, reference our Print and eBook Bulk Sales web page at www.apress.com/bulk-sales.

Any source code or other supplementary material referenced by the author in this book is available to readers on GitHub via the book's product page, located at https://github.com/Apress/Practical-Highcharts-with-Angular-2nd-edition-By-Sourabh-Mishra. For more detailed information, please visit www.apress.com/source-code.

Printed on acid-free paper

*This book is dedicated to
my Baba, Amma, Pappa, Mummy, Surbhee, Amar, Bhavya, and our
little rock star, Sarvagya.*

Table of Contents

About the Author

 **Sourabh Mishra** is an entrepreneur, developer, speaker, international author, corporate trainer, and animator. He is a Microsoft guy; he is very passionate about Microsoft technologies and is a true .NET warrior. Sourabh started his career when he was just 15 years old. He's loved computers from childhood. His programming experience includes C/C++, ASP.NET, C#, VB.NET, WCF, SQL Server, Entity Framework, MVC, Web API, Azure, jQquery, Highcharts, and Angular. Sourabh has been awarded Microsoft Most Valuable Professional (MVP) status. He has the zeal to learn new technologies and likes to share his knowledge on several online community forums.

He is a founder of "IECE Digital" and "Sourabh Mishra Notes," an online knowledge-sharing platform where one can learn new technologies very easily and comfortably.

He can be reached at

YouTube: sourabhmishranotes

Facebook: facebook.com/sourabhmishranotes

Twitter: sourabh_mishra1

Instagram: sourabhmishranotes

Email: sourabh_mishra1@hotmail.com

About the Technical Reviewer

Kenneth Fukizi is a software engineer, architect, and consultant with experience in coding on different platforms internationally. Prior to dedicated software development, he worked as a lecturer for a year and was then head of IT at different organizations. He has domain experience working with technology for companies in a wide variety of sectors. When he's not working, he likes reading up on emerging technologies and strives to be an active member of the software community.

Investment in knowledge is the biggest investment and sharing knowledge is the biggest service to society.

—Vinay Bharti Jain

Acknowledgments

Practical Highcharts with Angular has been a very special project, brought together through the efforts of very special people in my life. I am deeply thankful to the Apress team and to all those whose enthusiasm and energy transformed my vision to bring this book into reality, especially my family. Their commitment and sense of mission moved me to the next level.

I express my special thanks to:

- My wonderful parents, Shailendra Mishra and Saroj Mishra, who have supported me in every phase of my life and guided me from day one and gave me chance to work on computers in my childhood. My parents taught me to take challenges in life and come out successfully.

- My lovely and wise sister, Surbhee Mishra, a great marketer, and my brother-in-law Amar, for thier encouragement and support at every step.

- My wife, Bhavya, for her continuous support and love, and our little star Sarvagya, whose smile always makes my day.

- My uncle, Vinay Bharti Jain, who has always stood with me like a shield and guided me very well in critical decision making from the start of my career. My aunt, Poonam Jain, who has always believed that one day I will change the world through my knowledge.

- Naveen Verma, a great software architect and my teacher, who taught me how to write good code and how to use the right weapon at the right place in the world of software development.

- John Ebenezer, a wonderful human being and a true leader, who knows the art of people management. I learned from him how to deal with business people and get the best from the team.

- Welmoed Spahr, and the entire Apress/Springer team, for immediately evaluating the potential of this book and for believe in me and for making this book a reality. I sincerely value her guidance.

- Divya Modi, Shobana Srinivasan, Mark Powers, and James Markham for having faith in me, for bringing out this book, and for giving support, help, and guidance at every step during the entire journey of writing this book.

- My millions of readers across the globe who have encouraged me to write technical blogs and have given their love and affection, and also the people who are reading this book right now.

- Last but not least, with the deepest gratitude I wish to thank every person who has come into my life and has inspired, touched, and illuminated me through their presence.

Happy Reading!

Introduction

First of all, thank you for picking up this book. Whether you are standing in a bookshop or reading this at your office or at home, I assume that you probably have a strong interest in developing stunning and interactive dashboards for your web product.

Highcharts is a new-age tool for developing an interactive dashboard for your web products. You can easily define and use your data collection and get stunning graphs based on your requirements. In the second edition, we use the latest version of Highcharts and angular, plus the sunburst chart, the deviation chart, Bubble Series Chart, Dependency Wheel, Error Bar Series and many new charts. Nowadays, charting is used in finance, education, entertainment, sports, and real estate sectors to analyze data. Highcharts is built on top of modern JavaScript frameworks like jQuery and Angular. Highcharts enables developers to easily construct charts that will work in all modern browsers with pure knowledge of HTML, CSS, and JavaScript.

Who Should Read This Book

Practical Highcharts with Angular is a book mainly for developers/software architects. In this book, developers will learn step by step how to create client-side and server-side applications with the use of Angular with Highcharts and a REST-based API.

Organization of This Book

Each chapter in this book has been developed to highlight the powerful features of Highcharts. The following is brief summary of each chapter:

- **Chapter 1** gives you an introduction to Highcharts. If you are new to Highcharts, this is the place to start. You will learn the basics of charting, how to set up and install Highcharts for your application, and how to easily construct your first chart.

- **Chapter 2** talks about Scalable Vector Graphics and how to choose the right chart based on your requirements, because choosing the right chart (and setting the layout and legends) is an art.

- **Chapter 3** is the base for the rest of the chapters because here you will learn to develop an Angular app from the beginning. You will also learn the basics of Angular and how easily you can develop interactive charts using Highcharts.

- **Chapter 4** shows how to develop advanced charts with Angular and Highcharts, such as drilldowns, histograms, heatmaps, gauges, stacked bars, and more.

- **Chapter 5** shows how to get real-time data from the server side using REST-based services and how easily you can develop a client-side app using Angular and Highcharts.

- **Chapter 6** teaches you how to apply themes and layouts to a chart so it looks stunning and interactive. You also learn advanced concept of Highcharts like 3D, exporting in different formats, Pareto charts, combined charts, sunburst charts, deviation charts, error bar series, dependency wheel, bubble series chart and more.

- **Chapter 7** shows project-based learning. In this chapter, you will develop a project that offers a stunning and interactive dashboard with multiple charts. Here, you will get live NASDAQ historical data from the stock market using a REST API and then you will develop a dashboard based on a portfolio. With this app you can also track your real portfolio on the stock market, where you can track the top gainer and looser plus profit loss using Highcharts and Angular using the .NET Web API.

Source Code

All source code used in this book can be downloaded from github.com/Apress/Practical-Highcharts-with-Angular-2nd-edition-By-Sourabh-Mishra.

CHAPTER 1

Getting Started with Highcharts

Sourabh Mishra[a*]

[a] IECE Digital, Bangalore, India

Highcharts is a JavaScript-based library. You can use it to develop professional, high-quality, animated, web-based charting with minimal coding. Highcharts provides very simple built-in options that are easy to learn and easy to use; you just have to input data based on your data collection and it will give you charts based on your requirements.

Highcharts provides fast rendering and quick-to-deliver products. You can think out of the box and develop your charting very easily. Highcharts lets you call your services and use it with all modern JavaScript frameworks like Angular, jQuery, and others. You can export your charts into images, CSV files, or Excel files very easily. These built-in options are available at the time of development.

In this chapter, you are going to learn how to configure Highcharts into your web application. In the next part, you will learn how to implement charts very quickly.

Highcharts is built in such a way that all you have to do is input a collection of data and Highcharts will professionally render a chart for you.

Benefits of Highcharts

Highcharts is an excellent product for building charting for real-time applications. It provides the following rich benefits:

- It's easy to learn and easy to use. All you need is some knowledge of HTML, CSS, and JavaScript and you can develop your charts.

- It works in all modern browsers.

S. Mishra, *Practical Highcharts with Angular*, https://doi.org/10.1007/978-1-4842-9181-8_1

- It works in modern JavaScript libraries like Angular, Vue, React, and jQuery.

- You can export charts in various formats. Highcharts provides different charting types like line, bar, column, map, area, plot, stock, box, heat map, tree map, funnel, and scatter plot.

- It's an excellent tool for developing a real-time informative dashboard for your application.

- **Licenses**: Highcharts provides two types of licenses:

  1. **Non-commercial license:**

     This type of licensing is for non-profit purposes and personal use.

  2. **Commercial license:**

     This is for commercial purposes, such as an organization building products for commercial-level use.

You can go for a single website, developer license, or High-five license.

A single website license is for traditional websites. The developer license is for web apps and SaaS projects, and it comes in single dev, five dev, ten dev, etc.

History of Highcharts

Back in 2003, charting was not easily performed. People resorted to charting with the use of an HTML image or Java applet and servlet or Flash-based animated graphics charts. These products ruled the market. In 2009, Highsoft, a Norwegian-based company founded by Torstein Hønsi, developed and introduced a JavaScript-based framework to easily plug into enterprise products to generate world-class, stunning graphs based on your requirements.

Basics of Charting

A graph is a way to represent relationships between two or more related data. Every graph has two lines, vertical and horizontal (Figure 1-1). The horizontal graph line is called the *x-axis*, and the vertical line is called the *y-axis*. The point where these lines intersect each other is called the *origin point*. In the origin point, in the x-axis, the right side of the origin uses positive numbers and the left side uses negative numbers. The same thing happens with the y-axis: the value on the top side of the origin is positive and the downside is negative. The origin point value is always 0.

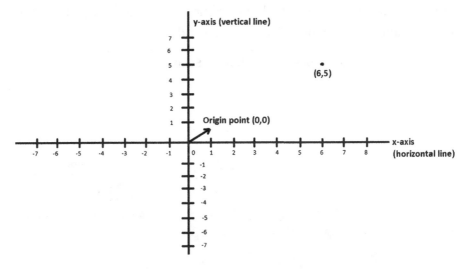

Figure 1-1. *A simple graph presentation for the x-axis and y-axis with data*

Figure 1-1 clearly shows the x-axis (horizontal) and y-axis (vertical). The right-hand side of the axis is positive; the left-hand side is negative. You can see the same for the y-axis.

Whenever you want to connect values of the x-axis and the y-axis, this point is called a *coordinate point*. In Figure 1-1, the value of x is 6 and y is 5, so the x and y coordinate is (6,5).

The following are the essential parts of every graph:

- **Title**: It describes what the graph is about.

- **Independent variable**: This part is defined by the x-axis. It usually indicates things like subject name, cricket overs, or temperatures, for example.

3

- **Dependent variable**: This part is defined by the y-axis. This part is connected with an independent variable, and it will show you the result because of the value of the independent variable, such as marks in an examination or cricket runs.

- **Scales**: This part decides where to plot points, which represent data. The scale always starts with 0 and increases with intervals, such as 3, 6, 9, 12, 15. It depends on data values.

- **Legend**: This is a short description of the graph's data.

Figure 1-2 shows a score by the St. Thomas School cricket team, including the title, independent variable, dependent variable, and legend.

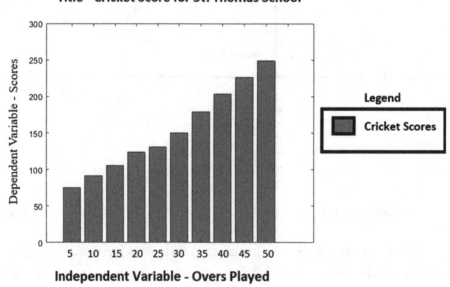

Figure 1-2. *A simple bar graph showing the essential parts of a chart*

It's now time to configure Highcharts into your web application and then quickly implement it.

Setup and Configuration

The installation of Highcharts into a web application is straightforward. You can configure and install Highcharts in three ways into your web application.

1. **CDN** (content delivery network): If you want to implement Highcharts with jQuery, you can use the CDN.

   ```
   <script src="https://code.jquery.com/jquery-3.4.1.min.js">
   </script>
   <script src="https://code.highcharts.com/highcharts.js">
   </script>
   ```

2. **Download the Highcharts.js file**: For this method, go to www. highcharts.com, open the download section, and download the latest zip file for Highcharts. Unzip and add a folder into your project file system.

   Add the following code based on your path to a file:

   ```
   <script src="code/highcharts.js"></script>
   ```

   The benefit with this method is that, without the Internet, you can run your project in a localhost environment.

3. **With a NuGet package**: If you are developing your project in Visual Studio or Visual Studio code, you can download the NuGet package. Here are the steps: right-click the project and select "Manage NuGet package" from the menu. You will get a dialog box. Click the Browse tab, type "Highcharts," and press Enter. See Figure 1-3.

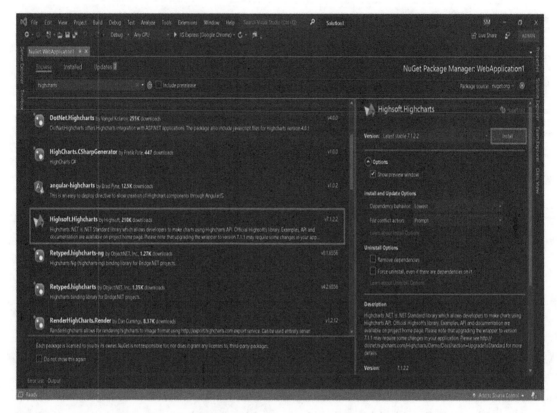

Figure 1-3.   *Installing Highcharts from the NuGet package*

As seen in Figure 1-3, you get a list in the Browse tab. In this list, select Highsoft. Highchart and click the Install button.

Click the OK button and select the I Accept button (Figure 1-4).

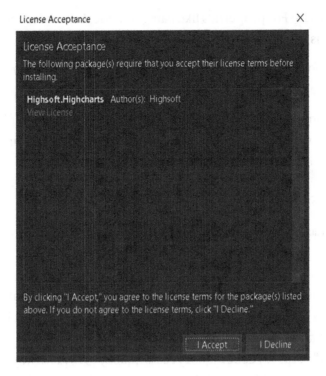

Figure 1-4. *Accepting a license for Highcharts from NuGet*

Now click Reference from Solution Explorer and you will get Highcharts added into a reference part.

Now you know the three ways to add Highcharts into your project.

Creating Your First Chart

Now it's time to do some hands-on with Highcharts. All Highcharts graphs mostly use the same configuration. Here are some significant properties that are always required in order to build Highcharts:

- chart: This property applies to the top-level setting. It can be the type of graph, where to render it in the page, layout of the chart, animations, and such.

- title/subtitle: For the chart title and subtitle

- xAxis/yAxis: For properties like category, title, CSS style, and interval for an axis

- series: For configuring the data collection to show in the graph, where you can set single or multiple series data

For the first example, you will learn how to generate a column graph. Listing 1-1 is an HTML file that you are going to add jQuery and Highcharts CDN, and then render a column-type graph into an HTML <div>.

Listing 1-1. Index.html

```
1. <!DOCTYPE html>
2. <html>
3. <head>
4. <meta http-equiv="Content-Type" content="text/html; charset=utf-8">
5. <meta name="viewport" content="width=device-width, initial-scale=1">
6. <title>Highcharts Example</title>
7. <script src="https://code.jquery.com/jquery-3.4.1.min.js"></script>
8. <script src="https://code.highcharts.com/highcharts.js"></script>
9. </head>
10. <body>
11. <div id="container"style="min-width: 310px; height: 400px;
    margin: 0auto"></div>
12. <script type="text/javascript">
13. var charts = new Highcharts.Chart({
14. chart: {
15. renderTo: 'container',
16. type: 'column'
17. },
18. title: {
19. text: 'Monthly Sales Chart Department Wise'
20. },
21. subtitle: {
22. text:'Year 2018'
23. },
24. xAxis: {
```

```
25. categories: [
26. 'Jan',
27. 'Feb',
28. 'Mar',
29. 'Apr',
30. 'May',
31. 'Jun',
32. 'Jul',
33. 'Aug',
34. 'Sep',
35. 'Oct',
36. 'Nov',
37. 'Dec'
38. ],
39. },
40. yAxis: {
41. min: 0,
42. title: {
43. text: 'Sales in Million $'
44. }
45. },
46. series: [{
47. name: 'Marketing Department',
48. data: [49.9, 51.5, 32.0, 82.0, 75.0, 66.0, 32.0, 25.0, 35.4, 65.1,
    58.6, 34.4]
49. },
50. {
51. name: 'Computer Science Department',
52. data: [40.5, 34.5, 84.4, 39.2, 23.2, 45.0, 55.6, 18.5, 26.4, 14.1,
    23.6, 84.4]
53. }]
54. });
55. </script>
56. </body>
57. </html>
```

If you run the above code, you will get the output shown in Figure 1-5.

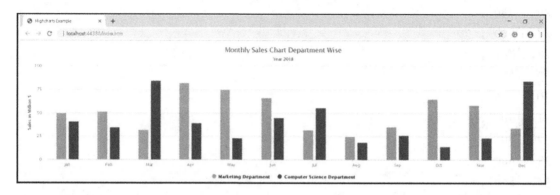

Figure 1-5. *Demo of your first bar chart*

Now, let's take a closer look at the code. This code has three parts. In the first part, you add jQuery and Highcharts CDN into the <head> portion:

```
<script src="https://code.jquery.com/jquery-3.4.1.min.js"></script>
<script src="https://code.highcharts.com/highcharts.js"></script>
```

Next, in the <body> section, there is a <div>. The reason for creating this <div> is that Highcharts will render in it.

```
<div id="container" style="min-width: 310px; height: 400px; margin: 0
auto"></div>
```

The next part of the code is Highcharts and JavaScript code. Let's understand it line by line.

The following line creates a new Highcharts object, and this object will define all the required properties, which are helpful to render a graph into the browser:

```
var charts = new Highcharts.Chart
```

The next line of code contains a property called renderTo, which indicates in the HTML page which particular <div> id you want to render this chart. The type property defines what type of graph you want to see, so in the type property, you can set line bar, spline, and so on.

```
var charts = new Highcharts.Chart({
chart: {
renderTo: 'container',
```

```
type: 'column'
    },
```

In the next line, you set the title and subtitle, so once your graph has rendered, your users will see whatever title/subtitle you want to show.

```
title: {
text: 'Monthly Sales Chart Department Wise'
      },
subtitle: {
text:'Year 2018'
      },
```

The next line is the `categories` property of the xAxis. It contains an array of labels for each data point.

```
xAxis: {
categories: [
'Jan',
'Feb',
'Mar',
'Apr',
'May',
'Jun',
'Jul',
'Aug',
'Sep',
'Oct',
'Nov',
'Dec'
],
  }
```

Next is the yAxis. Here the `min` property is related to setting a minimum value for a chart, so if you set as 0, Highcharts will never set for negative numbers. In the future, if any negative values come into the `series` collection, the chart will not show negative chart data points. If you want to work with negatives values, you can set `min` as -50 (or whatever highest min value you have) or you can remove it. In the yAxis area you can see negative data points.

The `title` property is used to set the title for the yAxis.

```
yAxis: {
min: 0,
title: {
text: 'Sales in Million $'
    }
    }
```

The next property is `series`, which is one of the most essential properties of Highcharts. First is `name` and it defines what type of data collection you are setting. This is also helpful for tooltips; when users hover their mouse pointer in a graph, it shows that this data point is related to a name. This is also helpful to set legends about the graph.

The `data` property refers to the collection of data in the form of an array, a series you can set as single or multiple. Later chapters will show you how to pass real-time data into a series section and render the chart.

```
series: [{
name: 'Marketing Department',
data: [49.9, 51.5, 32.0, 82.0, 75.0, 66.0, 32.0, 25.0, 35.4, 65.1,
58.6, 34.4]
    },
{
name: 'Computer Science Department',
data: [40.5, 34.5, 84.4, 39.2, 23.2, 45.0, 55.6, 18.5, 26.4, 14.1,
23.6, 84.4]
}]
```

Summary

Highcharts is a new-age tool for developing an interactive dashboard for your web products. You can easily define your data collection and get stunning graphs based on your requirements. In this chapter, you saw the basics of Highcharts and how easy it is to set up Highcharts and create your first column-type chart.

CHAPTER 2

Concept of Highcharts

Sourabh Mishra[a*]

[a] IECE Digital, Bangalore, India

In this chapter, you are going to learn the basic concepts of Highcharts and how it works. To use Highcharts, you must understand what type of chart to use based on your requirements. Then I will discuss some essential properties of Highcharts. So, let's get into the second chapter.

Scalable Vector Graphics

Scalable Vector Graphics (SVG) is an XML-based vector image format. Here *scalable* means that it can be resized up or down in any dimension without a loss in quality. SVG is designed for two-dimensional graphics and supports interactive graphics and animation. The behavior of Scalable Vector Graphics is defined in an XML text file. The benefit with this is that Scalable Vector Graphics can be searched, scripted, indexed, and compressed very efficiently. SVG is supported in all modern browsers like Internet Explorer, Microsoft Edge, Google Chrome, Safari, Opera, and Firefox.

In 1999, the World Wide Consortium (W3C) developed SVG as the language of vector graphics. With the use of SVG, you can create shapes, example paths, and outlines consisting of lines and curves, text, and bitmap images. In SVG, you can apply CSS for styling and JavaScript for scripting.

For text, you can apply internationalization and localization for more accessibility. Highcharts is also SVG-driven, so you can generate high-quality charts with interactive graphics and animations (Figure 2-1).

© Sourabh Mishra 2023
S. Mishra, *Practical Highcharts with Angular*, https://doi.org/10.1007/978-1-4842-9181-8_2

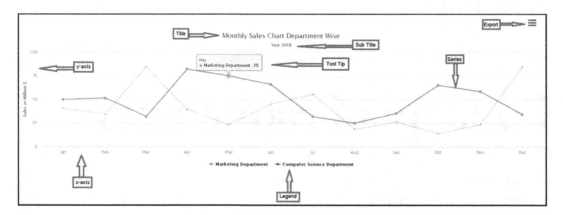

Figure 2-1. *SVG-based line chart presentation using Highcharts*

In Figure 2-1, the tooltip hovers and the first option you see is x-axis. In the x-axis, you draw months; the y-axis is where you populate values based on department revenue collection. These are pretty basic things. Then you have the title and subtitle for the graph, and then you plot a different data series based on revenue generation of departments. So, in the chart each one of the lines is a separate series. Then you have legends based on departments. There's a tooltip, and you can change your tooltip style based on the requirements. You can export into an image, CSV, or PDF.

Choosing the Right Chart Type Based on Requirements

Now let's talk about how to choose the right chart type. It's essential to understand the purpose of each kind of chart so that you can select the correct chart. Highcharts provides mainly four types of charts: bar charts, line charts, scatter plots, and maps. In later chapters, I will talk more about different charting types.

Bar Charts

Bar charts are a chart type that represents categorical data with rectangular bars in a proportion of height and length. These bars can plot horizontally or vertically. In bar charts, one axis may represent the specific categories being compared and the other axis may represent measured values.

Bar charts can be arranged in any order. In a bar chart, you can represent multiple data. When you want to represent values from highest to lowest incidents, this type of chart is called a Pareto chart. It provides a visual/graphical representation of categorical data. You can define categories like the age group of students, year, month, animals, or shoe size.

In column bar charts, these categories come in the x-axis horizontal form, and the height of the graph will generate based on values defined vertically on the y-axis.

When to Choose a Bar Chart

Bar charts are good for when you want to compare data based on categories, such as sales in a specific region or quarterly growth of a company (ex. Figure 2-2).

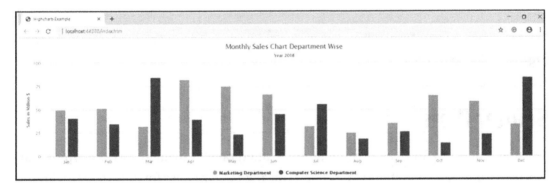

Figure 2-2. *Bar chart*

Line Charts

The line chart is also known as a line plot, line graph, or curve chart. It's a type of diagram that displays information in a series of data points. These data points are called markers, and these markers are connected by straight lines. The line chart is one of the standard charts used in many fields. The line chart is useful when you want to show a trend in data over an interval of time, or a time series; here the lines are drawn chronologically.

When to Choose a Line Chart

Line charts are suitable for a time series when you want to represent data in the form of a graph over time. Here you can define trend lines, and there are lots of ways to represent data over time and to make it meaningful so people can understand where things are going (Figure 2-3).

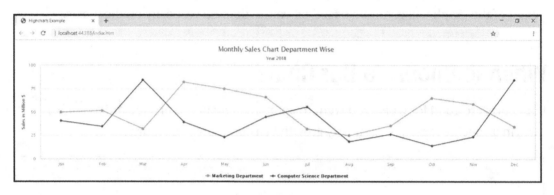

Figure 2-3. *Line chart*

Scatter Plots

A scatter plot, also known as a scatter graph, scattergram, or scatter chart, is a type of plot that uses Cartesian coordinates to display typically two variables for a set of data. Here points are coded and defined by color shape/size. Data is presented in the collection of points, and each point has one value.

Scatter plots come in a position of x-axis and y-axis, respectively. These types of graphs can show distributions very interestingly. A scatter plot designs for various kinds of correlations between variables with a specific confidence interval. For example, for weight and height, the weight would be on the y-axis and the height would be on the x-axis.

Suppose a university researcher is studying the capacity of lungs in a human body, specifically how long people can hold their breath. So, lung capacity is the first variable and time is the second variable. The researcher can plot data into a scatter plot, assigning lung capacity to the horizontal axis and length of time to the vertical axis.

Maps

Map charts allow you to represent your data on a geographical map. Here you can define the chart in two ways:

1. Graphical points

2. Geographical area

With geographic points, you can set your marks over geographical coordinates; these markers use color, shape, and size. The geographical area defines the colored area on the map. For example, an area could be a country, state, or city.

For example, in a world map, the United States, India, and Africa can be in different colors; each country indicates values. This type of map chart where we color geographical areas is known as a choropleth. In Highcharts, you can define detailing over maps, so when you click on the country, you can see the states of a nation, and when you click on states, you can see the cities. In later chapters, I will discuss maps in detail.

Setting Layouts

To set up the layout in Highcharts, the first step is to set a border around the plot area. For this you have five properties: `plotBorderWidth`, `plotBorderColor`, `borderColor`, `borderWidth`, and `border-radius` in the chart section (Figure 2-4).

```
chart: {
renderTo: 'container',
type: 'spline',
plotBorderColor: 'red',
plotBorderWidth: 1,
borderColor: 'grey',
borderWidth: 10,
borderRadius: 25
    },
```

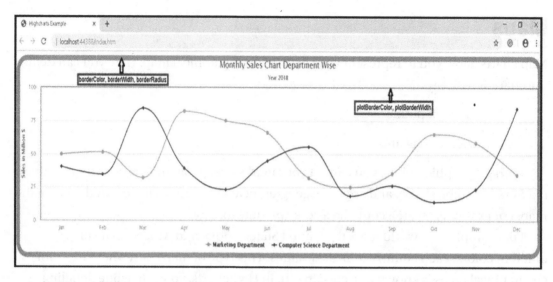

Figure 2-4. *Spline chart with a border layout*

Alignment

In Highcharts, you can set the alignment for labels such as title, subtitle, xAxis. title, yAxis.title, and credits. For alignment into Axis, you can set as high, middle, and low. For horizontal labels, you can set keywords such as left, center, and right.

In the world of charting, x is defined for horizontal and y is defined for vertical. You can set alignment through x and y positioning for the title and subtitle. For example, if you want the title and subtitle on one line, you can use the following code:

```
title: {
text: 'Monthly Sales Chart Department Wise',
align: 'left',
        },
subtitle: {
text: 'Year 2018',
align: 'right',
y: 15,
        }
```

In the above code, you set left align for the title and right for the subtitle. The positioning of y is 15, so by default the title position is 15; that's the reason both are on the same line. You can set the x value for the subtitle. If you set any value for x to 15, it will move more to the right (Figure 2-5).

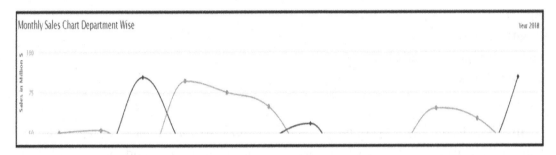

Figure 2-5. *Setting Highcharts title and subtitle alignment*

The verticalAlign property is used for setting the title and subtitle in the mode of the top, middle, and bottom.

```
title: {
text: 'Monthly Sales Chart Department Wise',
      },
subtitle: {
text: 'Year 2018',
verticalAlign: 'middle',
      }
```

Setting Up Chart Margins

You can set chart margins with four properties: marginTop, marginBottom, marginRight, and marginLeft. This will affect the overall layout of your chart. By default, these properties are not fixed, so you must set them. Once you set the margin properties, this will affect the plot area. The spacing effects are spacingTop, spacingBottom, spacingLeft, and spacingRight. Here marginTop sets the plot area top border, and this will also fix labels like the title and subtitle of the plot area. spacingLeft and spacingRight set the spacing areas.

Legends

You can set the alignment of legends in Highcharts very easily. There are three properties: align, verticalAlign, and layout.

```
legend: {
align: 'right',
verticalAlign: 'middle' ,
layout: 'vertical',
    },
```

In this code, the layout property is set as vertical, so the values of the legend are displayed vertically. Here the plot area automatically resizes for legends. verticalAlign is set to middle and aligns on the right-hand side (Figure 2-6).

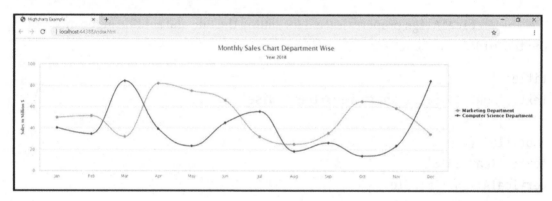

Figure 2-6. *Setting up the Highcharts legend alignment*

Setting Up Plot Lines

Every chart has a highest and lowest value. Suppose you must mark the highest and lowest index values. For this, plot lines are useful. Plot lines hold an array of object configurations for each plotline. For example, see this code and Figure 2-7:

```
plotLines: [{
width: 1,
value: 84.4,
color: 'red',
label: {
```

```
text: 'Highest Sale : 84.4',
style: {
color: 'green'
            }
        }
    },
        {
width: 1,
value: 14.1,
color: 'red',
label: {
text: 'Lowest Sale : 14.1',
style: {
color: 'green'
            }
        }
    }]
```

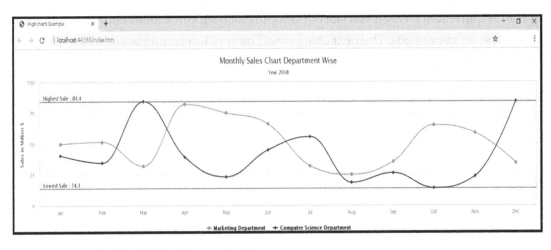

Figure 2-7. *Setting Highcharts plot lines*

As you can see, the plotLines properties have an array of configurations, and here you can provide index values. In the first index plot, you set your highest sale. You can set your labels with a style, and then you have another index for the lowest value.

Setting Credits

By default, the credit property is set as HighCharts.com. If you want to change this label, you can use the `credit` property. The `credit` object supports `align` and `verticalAlign`. The following is an example:

```
credits: {
position: {
align: 'center'
        },
text: 'Sourabh Mishra Notes',
      href: 'http://www.apress.com/'
      }
```

Summary

Highcharts supports Scalable Vector Graphics internally so you can resize your charts very quickly. With the use of Highcharts, you can design and configure your charts based on your requirements. When you start developing a chart, you should know what chart type is best for your needs. The next chapter will be very interesting because you will learn how to set up your application for Highcharts with Angular.

CHAPTER 3

Integrating Highcharts with Angular

Sourabh Mishra[a*]

[a] IECE Digital, Bangalore, India

In this chapter, you will learn the basics of Angular and how to configure and integrate Highcharts with Angular. Angular with Highcharts is a great combination.

What Is Angular?

Angular is designed to build single page applications. Angular makes your HTML more powerful and fast. HTML is known for its tags and static web development, but with Angular, you can apply local variables, loops, and if-else conditions. Angular provides two-way model data binding. Angular is a product of Google and is top rated by millions of web developers.

Angular provides validations, routing, and binding, which makes developer life more comfortable, so you can build your apps faster. You can easily display your data fields from the data model, track your changes, and process updates from the user. Angular provides a modular approach by its design.

Every web app has a set of building blocks, and every app connects with different modules. Angular makes content easy to develop, and you can create reusable code through components. Angular easily connects with back-end web services; with the use of this feature, Angular apps easily connect with HTTP get and HTTP post data to execute server-side business logic.

© Sourabh Mishra 2023

S. Mishra, *Practical Highcharts with Angular*, https://doi.org/10.1007/978-1-4842-9181-8_3

Angular is born for speed and for improving your web apps. It provides faster initial loads, improved page render times, and quick change detection. Angular is a modern framework with rich features and the latest JavaScript standards. Angular supports all modern browsers. Angular is a simple and rich JavaScript framework, and it provides built-in directives and two-way data binding. It is easy to learn and easy to use, and this improves your productivity in your day-to-day work.

You will get productivity improvement when you interact with Highcharts projects in later chapters.

What's New in Angular

Angular started as AngularJs in 2010. Later, Google decided to rewrite this framework with powerful libraries and thus Angular 2.0 was created in 2016. It was a revolution in the field of single page application development. Today key improvements include support for progressive web apps, which is good for hybrid mobile app development.

The following are the new and key features of Angular:

- HttpClient is a powerful, smart, and easy-to-use library for making HTTP requests for API calls.

- Angular 9 onwards comes up with the IVY compiler, IVY Compiler is the latest compiler for Angular application released by Angular Team. Currently, Angular is using View Engine compiler to compile Angular application, which offers many advantages, such as

  - Faster testing

  - Smart and small bundling

  - Improved CSS

  - New AOT (ahead of time) builder, which improves build time

  - Improved internationalization

  - New date range picker

  - Improved output bundle size and increased development speed

Configuring Angular

To configure Angular in your system, you have to set up a development environment with the following applications:

- Node.js

- Code editor

- Angular CLI

Setting Up Node.js

Node.js is a free, open source server environment that provides cross-platform features so you can use Windows, Linux, and macOS. Node.js uses JavaScript so it's straightforward to build services using it. Node.js provides an extensive ecosystem for open source libraries. Developers prefer Node.js because they can quickly scale up their development in any direction. Node.js is useful for developing real-time, complex, single page applications.

To install Node.js on your system, download it from `https://nodejs.org/en/download/`. Once you open this site, you'll see the screen shown in Figure 3-1.

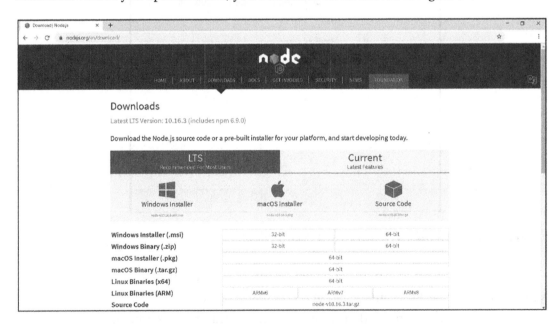

Figure 3-1. *Download screen from the Node.js website*

Figure 3-1 shows how to download Node.js based on your operating system. Once your download is complete, install the .exe file on your system (Figures 3-2 and 3-3).

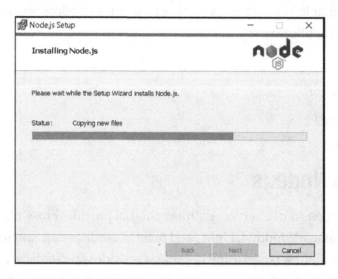

Figure 3-2. *Installing Node.js*

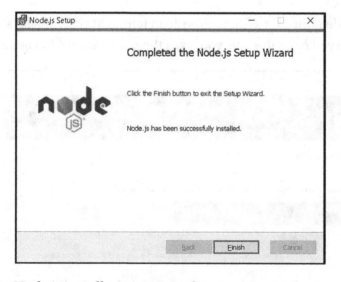

Figure 3-3. *The Node.js installation is complete*

After your installation is done, you can see the Node.js command prompt in your system. Click Start ➤ Programs ➤ Node.js command prompt.

Open the Node.js command prompt with administrator rights and type the command npm -v (Figure 3-4).

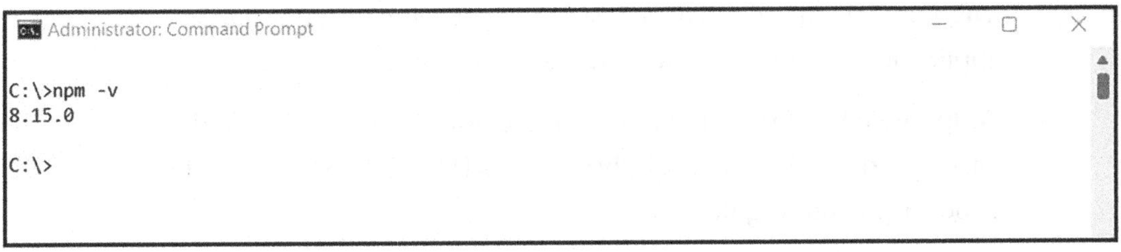

Figure 3-4. *Node.js command prompt screen*

After running npm-v, you'll see the current version of your npm.

Code Editor

The code editor is designed to simplify and speed up the writing of source code via syntax, indentation, auto-complete, and brace matching functionality. Code editors are responsible for debugging, building, and compiling your code. These editors also provide code extensions for different programming languages.

In this book, we will work mostly in Visual Studio code. Visual Studio code is developed by Microsoft. Visual Studio code provides cross-platform features so it can run easily on the Windows, macOS, and Linux operating systems. You can think beyond syntax highlighting and autocomplete with IntelliSense, which provides smart completion based on function definitions, variable types, and imported modules. Visual Studio code provides a rich debugging feature form editor. You can insert a break point, attach processes very easy for debugging, and understand the system. You can deploy your code over the cloud very quickly. Visual Studio code also supports Git and other SCM providers.

It's a free code editor. You can download it from https://code.visualstudio.com/download.

Here is a list of other code editors you can download based on your preference:

- **Microsoft Visual Studio IDE**: Developed by Microsoft, it's designed for developing web applications, console-based applications, mobile applications, GUIs, services, and more. It supports many programming languages like C#, Java, C++, VB, Python, JavaScript, and TypeScript.

- **Angular IDE**: Angular IDE is designed to develop Angular-based applications. It supports JavaScript and TypeScript.

- **WebStorm**: WebStorm is a powerful tool for developing JavaScript-based products. WebStorm fully supports HTML, CSS, JavaScript, TypeScript, and Angular.

- **Bluefish**: Bluefish is a code editor for programmers and web developers. Bluefish is a very lightweight code editor, and it supports all modern programming languages. It's fast and supports work on multiple projects. Bluefish offers auto recovery of code, an inline spell checker, a character map for Unicode characters, and site upload features.

Setting Up Angular CLI

The Angular command-line interface (CLI) is developed for automating operations for Angular projects. It saves developers time and effort. With the use of the Angular CLI, you can configure and set up your development environment. The Angular CLI is helpful for building services, components, routing, and projects, and it helps them compile and run faster.

The first step is to set up and install the Angular CLI. To run the following command in Visual Studio code, click the Terminal menu ➤ New Terminal. Then type the following command (as seen in Figure 3-5):

```
npm install -g @angular/cli
```

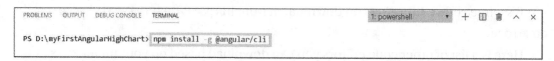

Figure 3-5. *Installing the Angular CLI through the terminal window of VS code*

Here –g stands for global installation. You are using it so in the future you can call the CLI in Angular projects quickly.

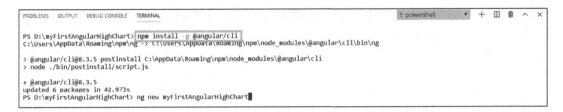

Figure 3-6. *Installation completed for the Angular CLI*

Once the npm installation for the Angular CLI is completed (Figure 3-6), it's time to create a new Angular application. To create/generate a new Angular application, type the following command:

ng new application-name

In this demo, you are going to create an application named myFirstAngularHighChart. Type the following command (Figure 3-7):

ng new myFirstAngularHighChart

Figure 3-7. *Creating/generating a new Angular application*

Once you press Enter, the CLI will ask you some questions. The first one is if you would like to add Angular routing. Press Y and press Enter.

When it comes to picking which stylesheet format you would like to use, here you can set CSS or SCSS based on your requirements. In this application, you will work with CSS. Press Enter (Figure 3-8).

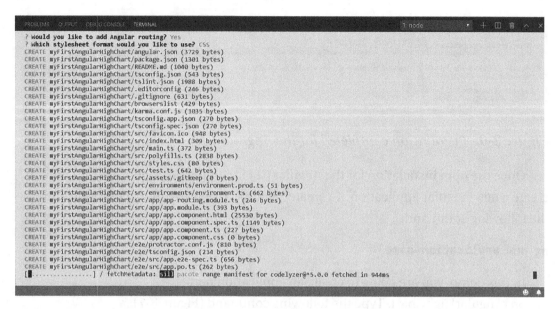

Figure 3-8. *Creating a new Angular application*

Now a process will start. It will take a few minutes to install your Angular application (Figure 3-9).

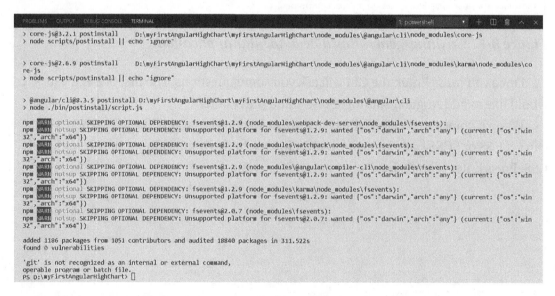

Figure 3-9. *Angular application generation completed screen*

If you see the screen shown in Figure 3-9, the Angular creation process is done. Go to File ➤ Open Folder, select Folder, and click Open. On the left-hand side, you can see that the CLI generated your application folder structure. Now it's time to understand the Angular application structure (Table 3-1).

Table 3-1. *Application Structure of an Angular App*

Folders/Config Files	Use
e2e	End-to-end test files. The e2e folder contains a source file for testing.
node_modules	This folder contains npm packages for an entire application. Project dependencies also reside here.
Src	In this folder, you will get application-level source code like modules, HTML, components, application-level environment config files, icon files, and the main page index file.
.editorconfig	Configuration for code editors
.gitignore	This configuration file will intentionally untrack that Git should ignore.
angular.json	Here you can set the default configuration for a build, serve, testing, index page, styles, tsconfig, and more.
package.json	Here you will get all required project dependencies with their versioning. Whenever you add a new dependency for your project, you will get entries here.
tsconfig.json	TypeScript configuration file for the entire app
tslint.json	Default configuration file for tslint

Now I will talk about some essential things that are required to work in Angular with Highcharts.

TypeScript

TypeScript is an open-source programming language developed by Anders Hejlsberg at Microsoft. After compilation internally, TypeScript is converted to JavaScript. TypeScript is a pure strongly typed and object-oriented language; here you can create classes and an interface like in C# and Java. Angular with TypeScript is a great combination.

Now it's time to configure Highcharts with the Angular application. For this, open a project and go to the Visual Studio code terminal window and type the following command:

```
npm install highcharts
```

This command will add Highcharts dependencies to your project.

Highcharts Angular Wrapper

The Highcharts angular wrapper is open source. It provides vibrant and dynamic feature visualization for Highcharts within an Angular application. This wrapper offers browser compatibility for all modern browsers like IE, Chrome, Safari, and Mozilla. A Highcharts wrapper API is available and supports TypeScript.

To install this wrapper, run the following command in the terminal window:

```
npm install highcharts-angular
```

Now open the package.json file. You can see in the package list new entries for Highcharts. This shows that your Highcharts dependencies are correctly installed, and now you can use them in your application.

In the Angular application, if you go to the src ➤ app folder, you will get the following files:

- app-routing.module.ts: This file is responsible for routing.

- app.module.ts: Here, the root module is defined; in this file, all related components and dependencies will be added for a module (Listing 3-1).

- app.component.ts: This is a component. Here you write business logic and set a selector for the HTML template and models for binding (Listing 3-2).

- app.component.html: This is an HTML page for components. Here you can call your logic methods and bind models (Listing 3-3).

- app.component.css: Here you can add your base CSS style sheet for root code.

- app.component.spec.ts: Here you can set a unit test for the root component.

Start by adding some code into `app.module.ts`, as shown in Listing 3-1.

Listing 3-1. app.module.ts

```
import { BrowserModule } from '@angular/platform-browser';
import { NgModule } from '@angular/core';
import { AppRoutingModule } from './app-routing.module';
import { AppComponent } from './app.component';
import { HighchartsChartModule } from 'highcharts-angular';

@NgModule({
  declarations: [
    AppComponent,

  ],
  imports: [
    BrowserModule,
    AppRoutingModule,
     HighchartsChartModule
  ],
  providers: [],
  bootstrap: [AppComponent]
})
export class AppModule { }
```

Let's try to understand the above code line by line:

- import: Angular modules/components are written in the TypeScript language using the export keyword, so in order to refer to these components/modules, you must refer to the import statement. The syntax to import is

  `import {module/component} from 'path of the file system.'`

- BrowserModule: This exports all required infrastructure for an Angular app.

- @angular/platform-browser: This executes Angular apps to all supported browsers.

- NgModule: NgModule is a class that contains the @NgModule decorator.
  It's responsible for adding dependent components.

- @angular/core: This is responsible for implementing Angular core
  functionality, utilities, and low-level services.

- AppRoutingModule: This belongs to app-routing.module.ts and is
  responsible for routing and navigation for the Angular app.

- AppComponent: AppComponent is a class declared in app.component.ts.
  You can create a class with a different name.

- HighchartsChartComponent: This is for Highcharts. This is a class,
  and here you are adding this dependency to your Angular app.

- @NgModule: The ngmodule configures the module and injects related
  dependencies. ngmodule is a decorator that declares appcomponent
  and highchartcomponent and imports modules, bootstrapping the
  main component. Here *bootstrap* is a term for kick-starting your app,
  so whenever your application is going to run, bootstrap will initialize
  a component, and that component will run its related HTML into the
  browser.

- export: In Angular, whenever you define a class, and you want to use
  this class in different modules, you must define it as export; it's the
  same as the public keyword in Java and C#.

Now copy the code in Listing 3-2 into app.component.ts.

Listing 3-2. app.components.ts

```
import { Component } from '@angular/core';
import * as Highcharts from 'highcharts';
@Component({
  selector: 'app-root',
  templateUrl: './app.component.html',
  styleUrls: ['./app.component.css']
})
```

```
export class AppComponent {
  title = 'myHighChartsApp';
  Highcharts: typeof Highcharts = Highcharts;
  chartOptions: Highcharts.Options = {
    chart: {
      type: "column"
    },
    title: {
      text: "Monthly Sales Chart Department Wise"
    },
    subtitle: {
      text: "Year 2022"
    },
    xAxis: {
      categories: ["Jan", "Feb", "Mar", "Apr", "May", "Jun",
        "Jul", "Aug", "Sep", "Oct", "Nov", "Dec"]
    },
    yAxis: {
      title: {
        text: "Sales in Million $"
      }
    },
    series: [{
      type: "column",
      name: 'Marketing Department',
      data: [49.9, 51.5, 32.0, 82.0, 75.0, 66.0, 32.0, 25.0,
             35.4, 65.1, 58.6, 34.4]
    },
    {
      type: "column",
      name: 'Computer Science Department',
      data: [40.5, 34.5, 84.4, 39.2, 23.2, 45.0, 55.6, 18.5,
             26.4, 14.1, 23.6, 84.4]
    }]
  };
}
```

In Listing 3-2, the @Component decorator helps create a fundamental building block for the UI. With this decorator, your class becomes a component. The component of Angular is a subset of directives. In the next line, you use three metadata properties.

- selector: selector is used to create tags to call in HTML. In this code, you use app-root so in HTML you will call this as

-

- templateUrl: The template URL is the relative UI path for the HTML template file.

- styleUrls: Here you can define a component CSS path. This is an array type. If you have multiple CSS files for this component, you can define them here.

The next line creates a class named AppComponent. And then you call the Highcharts JavaScript code. In the next step, you move the existing code into the app.component.html file and copy the code from Listing 3-3 into the app.component.html file.

Listing 3-3. app.component.html

```
<div class="content" role="main">
  <highcharts-chart [Highcharts]="Highcharts"
   [options]="chartOptions"
      style="width: 100%; height: 400px; display: block;">
   </highcharts-chart>
  </div>
  <router-outlet></router-outlet>
```

Let's explore the Listing 3-3 code. As you can see in the app.component.html code, you call a highcharts-chart directive in a <div>.

```
<highcharts-chart [Highcharts]="Highcharts"
   [options]="chartOptions"
      style="width: 100%; height: 400px; display: block;">
   </highcharts-chart>
```

Then there are two models, [Highcharts] and [options], so in app.component.ts, you define Highcharts and chartOptions as variables into the AppComponent class and define their values. In this HTML, you just bind those models.

So <highcharts-chart></highcharts-chart> is a calling directive and you have two models to bind, [Highcharts] and [options].

Listing 3-4 is the main index.html for your project. In it is one directive tag called <app-root></app-root>. In app.component.ts, in the selector metadata property, you define this as selector: 'app-root'.

Listing 3-4. index.html

```
<!doctype html>
<html lang="en">
<head>
  <meta charset="utf-8">
  <title>MyHighChartsApp</title>
  <base href="/">
  <meta name="viewport" content="width=device-width, initial-scale=1">
  <link rel="icon" type="image/x-icon" href="favicon.ico">
</head>
<body>
  <app-root></app-root>
</body>
</html>
```

Whenever this Angular app compiles and runs in the browser, it will check the <app-root> from the component decorator, and from there it will take the template URL of component.html, and then your component page will render.

To run this Angular app, open a new terminal from VS code, and type ng serve. Press Enter. By default, it gives the URL as localhost:4200. Now go to a browser and run this URL. Your app will run (Figure 3-10).

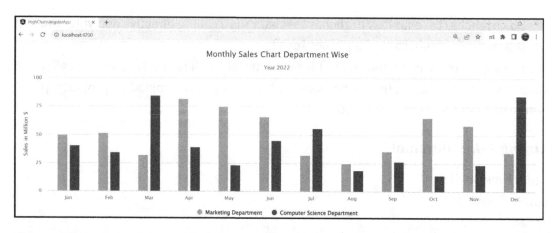

Figure 3-10. *Running an Angular app in a browser through ng serve*

If you want to change the chart type, go to `app.component.ts` and change its type (Listing 3-5).

Listing 3-5. app.component.ts

```
import { Component } from '@angular/core';
import * as Highcharts from 'highcharts';
@Component({
  selector: 'app-root',
  templateUrl: './app.component.html',
  styleUrls: ['./app.component.css']
})
export class AppComponent {
  title = 'myHighChartsApp';
  Highcharts: typeof Highcharts = Highcharts;
  chartOptions: Highcharts.Options = {
    chart: {
      type: "area"
    },
    title: {
      text: "Monthly Sales Chart Department Wise"
    },
```

```
    subtitle: {
      text: "Year 2021"
    },
    xAxis: {
      categories: ["Jan", "Feb", "Mar", "Apr", "May", "Jun",
        "Jul", "Aug", "Sep", "Oct", "Nov", "Dec"]
    },
    yAxis: {
      title: {
        text: "Sales in Million $"
      }
    },
    series: [{
      type: "area",
      name: 'Marketing Department',
      data: [49.9, 51.5, 32.0, 82.0, 75.0, 66.0, 32.0, 25.0, 35.4, 65.1,
      58.6, 34.4]
    },
    {
      type: "area",
      name: 'Computer Science Department',
      data: [40.5, 34.5, 84.4, 39.2, 23.2, 45.0, 55.6, 18.5, 26.4, 14.1,
      23.6, 84.4]
    }]
  };
}
```

Now run the ng serve command, and you will get the output shown in Figure 3-11.

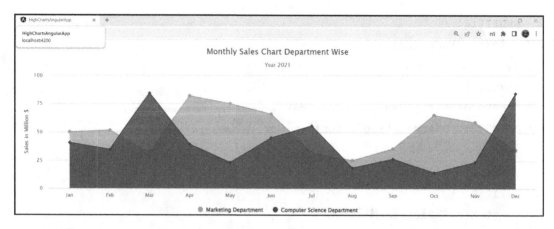

Figure 3-11. *The Angular app with an area chart*

Summary

Angular is a superset of JavaScript. Creating, building, compiling, and running an application through Angular is very easy. Angular provides faster execution, faster building, and agile development. Using Angular with Highcharts is a great combination. With Highcharts' Angular dependencies, you can develop stunning, beautiful charts very quickly. For large professional projects, Angular is very popular. In this chapter, you explored basic building blocks, which are required to create an Angular app with Highcharts. In the next chapter, you will see different charting types and how to utilize more of Highcharts with Angular and jQuery.

CHAPTER 4

Different Charting Types

Sourabh Mishra[a*]

[a] IECE Digital, Bangalore, India

In this chapter, you will learn about the different charting types you can develop with the use of Highcharts. This chapter will cover the different types of charts in detail and how you can apply them to your web application using Angular.

You will explore the following charts in this chapter:

- Pie chart

- Donut chart

- Drilldown chart

- Line chart

- Area chart

- Scatter chart

- Histogram chart

- Heatmap series chart

- Stacked bar chart

- Column pyramid chart

- Gauge chart

© Sourabh Mishra 2023
S. Mishra, *Practical Highcharts with Angular*, https://doi.org/10.1007/978-1-4842-9181-8_4

Pie Charts

In a pie chart, each slice of the pie describes how much data exists for it. Pie charts are mostly used in business, construction, media, and market research. For business, a pie chart may help to show business success or failure based on each product. You can also figure out the diet of a person with a pie chart. A benefit of the pie chart is there is no axis to con the data; only data with categories are required.

Let's start by creating a simple pie chart with Angular and Highcharts. In earlier chapters, you created the basic Angular configuration and an application. In this chapter, you will work on the component level only, so most of the work will be done in app.component.ts. For the creation of this component, you can refer to Chapter 3.

In this example, you are going to create a pie chart that describes various programming languages used by developers worldwide. See Listings 4-1 and 4-2.

Listing 4-1. piechart.component.ts

```
import { Component, OnInit } from '@angular/core';
import * as Highcharts from "highcharts";
@Component({
  selector: 'app-piechart',
  templateUrl: './piechart.component.html',
 styleUrls: ['./piechart.component.css']
})
export class PiechartComponent  {
  title = 'myHighChartsApp';
  highcharts = Highcharts;
  chartOptions: Highcharts.Options = {
    chart: {
      type: 'pie'
    },
    title: {
      text: 'Programming Languages used by developers worldwide'
    },
    plotOptions: {
      pie: {
        allowPointSelect: true,
```

```
      cursor: 'pointer',
      dataLabels: {
        enabled: true,
        format: '<b>{point.name}</b>: {point.percentage:.1f} %'
      }
    }
  },
  tooltip: {
  pointFormat: '{series.name}: <b>{point.percentage:.1f}%</b>'
  },
  series: [{
    type: "pie",
    name: 'Uses',
    colorByPoint: true,
    data: [{
      name: 'C#',
      y: 55,
      sliced: true,
      selected: true
    }, {
      name: 'VB',
      y: 25
    }, {
      name: 'J#',
      y: 10
    }, {
      name: 'VC++',
      y: 10
    }]
  }]
};
}
```

Listing 4-2. piechart.component.html

```
<div class="content" role="main">
    <highcharts-chart [Highcharts]="highcharts" [options]="chartOptions"
        style="width: 100%; height: 400px; display: block;">
    </highcharts-chart>
</div>
<router-outlet></router-outlet>
```

In this chapter, for all examples, the piechart.component.html code will be same (Listing 4-2); you only have to change code in piechart.component.ts (Listing 4-1).

To run this example, type ng serve and press Enter. You will get the output shown in Figure 4-1.

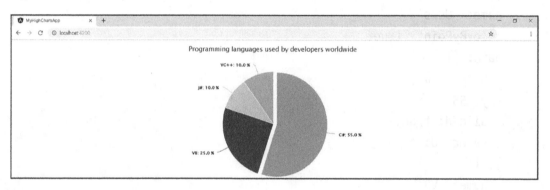

Figure 4-1. *Simple pie chart*

Now let's understand the code in the piechart.component.ts file. In the last chapter, I discuss the basics of Angular. Here I will talk about the Highcharts code.

In the piechart.component.ts code, you set the type property as pie so it creates a pie chart.

Now let's look at plotOptions. It is a wrapper object for the configuration for each series type:

```
plotOptions: {
   pie: {
     allowPointSelect: true,
     cursor: 'pointer',
     dataLabels: {
       enabled: true,
       format: '<b>{point.name}</b>: {point.percentage:.1f} %'
```

```
      }
    }
  }
```

Next, `allowPointSelect` is a Boolean type property. Here it's set to `true` so that the user can click over the chart to select and deselect that particular series in the chart. For example, in this chart, if the user clicks C# or VB, that specific slice will select and deselect based on the click. If it is set to `false`, this functionality will not work.

For `cursor`, whenever a mouse pointer hovers into a series, the `hand type` mouse pointer will appear if you set this `as cursor: 'pointer'`.

You can see data labels in each series. Here you must enable `dataLabels` to `true` so you can set the format of your data into labels. Figure 4-2 shows the data labels; in this example, red rectangles define the data labels.

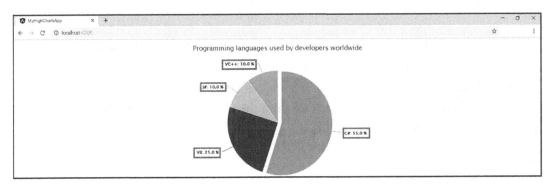

Figure 4-2. *The dataLables property in a pie chart*

If you want to set the legend in this particular pie chart, add `showInLegend: true`. You can set this property after the `allowPointSelect` property. The following is the code, and the chart is shown in Figure 4-3:

```
pie: {
    allowPointSelect: true,
    showInLegend: true,
    cursor: 'pointer',
    dataLabels: {
     enabled: true,
     format: '<b>{point.name}</b>: {point.percentage:.1f} %'
    }
}
```

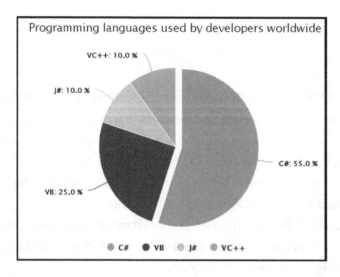

Figure 4-3. *A pie chart with legends*

The sliced0ffset property sets how far you want to move out the particular section of pie from the chart. By default, the value is set to 10, but you can increase it.

Next, sliced is a Boolean property. If it's set as true, based on the series where you are applying this property, it will slice it off from the pie chart (plus any offset you set) that much distance. Consider the following code:

```
pie: {
    allowPointSelect: true,
    showInLegend: true,
    slicedOffset:50,
    cursor: 'pointer',
    dataLabels: {
      enabled: true,
      format: '<b>{point.name}</b>: {point.percentage:.1f} %'
    }
  }
series: [{
    type: "pie",
    name: 'Uses',
    data: [{
      name: 'C#',
```

```
      y: 55,
      sliced: true,
      selected: true
   }
```

Run this code to display the chart shown in Figure 4-4.

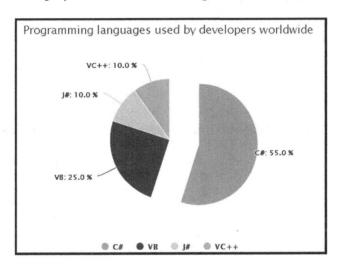

Figure 4-4. *A pie chart with the sliced and slicedOffset properties*

Donut Chart

A donut chart is another type of pie chart. It's useful when you want detailed information. The center hole in this chart makes it looks like a donut shape.

The next example shows how a donut chart is helpful for details. In this example, you will get the details on different JavaScript frameworks used by developers. This demo is just an example; it's not real data. I wish to show you how to develop a donut chart and make your life easier. Listing 4-3 shows the code.

Listing 4-3. donutchart.component.ts

```
import { Component, OnInit } from '@angular/core';
import * as Highcharts from 'highcharts';
@Component({
  selector: 'app-donutchart',
```

```
  templateUrl: './donutchart.component.html',
  styleUrls: ['./donutchart.component.css']
})
export class DonutchartComponent {
  highcharts = Highcharts;
  chartOptions: Highcharts.Options = {
    chart: {
      renderTo: 'container',
      type: 'pie'
    },
    title: {
      text: 'Javascript framework used by developers worldwide'
    },
    plotOptions: {
      pie: {
        innerSize: '60%'
      }
    },
    series:
      [
        {
          type:'pie',
          name: 'Uses',
          data: [
            ['AngularJs', 10.2],
            ['Angular', 20.7],
            ['JQuery', 10],
            ['Vue', 3.1],
            ['ReactJs', 5.4]
          ]
        }
      ]
  }
}
```

As you can see in Listing 4-3, one property is `innerSize:60%`; this property makes a hole in the pie chart, which gives it a donut design. You can increase or decrease it as per your requirements (Figure 4-5).

```
plotOptions: {
  pie: {
    innerSize: '60%'
  }
}
```

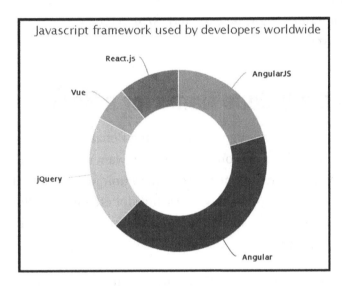

Figure 4-5. *Pie chart with donut feature*

Drilldown Charts

Drilldown charts provide an in-depth and detailed view of your chart. Highcharts provides a drilldown effect on the pie chart so you can get more details into your chart. To add a drilldown effect into your charts, you must add some dependencies in your code.

Required Dependencies

jQuery:

```
<script src="https://code.highcharts.com/highcharts-more.js"></script>
<script src="https://code.highcharts.com/modules/drilldown.js"></script>
```

Angular:

```
import More from 'highcharts/highcharts-more';
More(Highcharts);
import Drilldown from 'highcharts/modules/drilldown';
Drilldown(Highcharts);
```

Setting Up the Unique Name for a Series

Drilldown charts are basically designed for detailing a chart. In a series, suppose you have four types of information and on each click you want to see the details of that particular type, so you require unique names. These unique names are used to connect with a drilldown event. Listing 4-4 shows the syntax for creating a drilldown series and Listing 4-5 shows how to use the same unique names in the listing and get detailed information about the chart.

Listing 4-4. Creating a Series for a Drilldown Chart

```
series: [{
    type:'pie'
    name: 'Series Name',
    data: [
     {
      name: 'name of series',
      y: 62.12,
      drilldown: 'unique-name'
     },
     ['Data 1', value 1],
     ['Data 2', value 2],
```

```
    ['Data 3', value 3]
  ]
}],
```

Listing 4-5. Getting the Details on a Click for the Drilldown

```
drilldown: {
series: [{
type:'pie'
name: 'name of drill down series',
id: ' unique-name',
data: [
['Detail 1', value 1],
['Detail 2', value 2],
['Detail 3', value 3],
['Detail 4',value 4],
['Detail 5', value 5]
]
}]
```

In the upcoming example, you will draw a drilldown chart, which gives you in-depth details of JavaScript framework versions. If you click one framework, such as Angular, it will take you down one more layer in that particular series. Copy the complete code in Listing 4-6 and paste it into the drilldownchart.component.ts file.

Listing 4-6. drilldownchart.component.ts

```
import { Component, OnInit } from '@angular/core';
import * as Highcharts from 'highcharts';
import More from 'highcharts/highcharts-more';
More(Highcharts);
import Drilldown from 'highcharts/modules/drilldown';
Drilldown(Highcharts);

@Component({
  selector: 'app-drilldownchart',
  templateUrl: './drilldownchart.component.html',
  styleUrls: ['./drilldownchart.component.css']
})
```

```
export class DrilldownchartComponent {
  title = 'myHighChartsApp';
  highcharts = Highcharts;
  chartOptions: Highcharts.Options  = {
    chart: {
      type: 'pie',
    },
    title: {
      text: 'Pie Chart with drill down Feature'
    },
    plotOptions: {
      pie: {
        innerSize: 100,
      }
    },
    tooltip: {
headerFormat:'<span style="font-size:10px">{series.name}</span><br>',
pointFormat:'<span style="color:{point.color}">{point.name}</span>:
<b>{point.y:.2f}%</b> of total<br/>'
    },
    series: [{
      type:'pie',
      name: 'JavaScript Frameworks',
      data: [
        {
          name: 'Angular',
          y: 62.12,
          drilldown: 'angular-versions'
        },
        ['VueJs', 9.35],
        ['ReactJs', 15.89],
        ['Jquery', 12.64]
      ]
    }],
    drilldown: {
```

```
    series: [{
      type:'pie',
      name: 'Angular versions',
      id: 'angular-versions',
      data: [
        ['Angular Js', 17.07],
        ['Angular 2', 15],
        ['Angular 5', 16],
        ['Angular 8', 20.58],
        ['Angular 10', 27.35],
        ['Angular 14', 47.35]
      ]
    }]
  }
 }
}
```

Listing 4-6 provides a drilldown feature for the first series array only for Angular; the rest of the frameworks, like React, don't get the drilldown functionality. If you want to provide the drilldown effect, you must set the series as `drilldown: 'uniquename for the drilldown'`. This unique name is required because when you go into detailing this drilldown, the unique property name should match with the drilldown of the series array. You can add this drilldown feature into another series array. So always remember that the unique name should be different.

```
series: [{
  type:'pie',
  name: 'JavaScript Frameworks',
  data: [
   {
    name: 'Angular',
    y: 62.12,
    drilldown: 'angular-versions'
   },
   ['VueJs', 9.35],
   ['ReactJs', 15.89],
```

```
    ['Jquery', 12.64]
  ]
}],
```

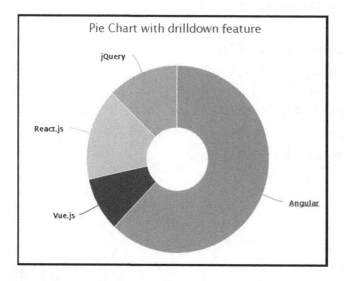

Figure 4-6. *Drilldown with pie feature*

Whenever you run this code, it will first look like Figure 4-6. Now let's go to the next level of the code:

```
drilldown: {
   series: [{
   type:'pie',
    name: 'Angular versions',
    id: 'angular-versions',
    data: [
      ['Angular Js', 17.07],
      ['Angular 2', 15],
      ['Angular 5', 16],
      ['Angular 8', 20.58],
      ['Angular 10', 27.35],
      ['Angular 14', 47.35]

    ]
   }]
  }
```

In this code, the drilldown id (`'angular-versions'`) matches your series drilldown property value; both ids are the same as the Angular versions. In this way Highcharts interacts within the features it has to call. In this example, once you click the Angular part, you will get Figure 4-7.

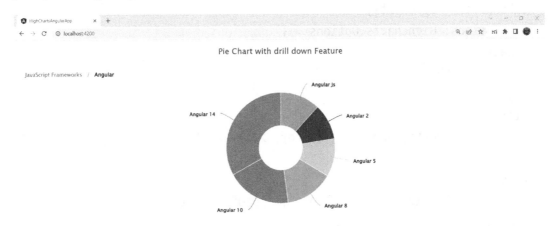

Figure 4-7. *Pie with drilldown detailed effect after you click the series*

In Figure 4-7, there is a button that comes automatically label as <Back to JavaScript Frameworks>. Clicking this button takes you to Figure 4-6. This is how you can implement drilldown effects into pie charts. I hope you enjoy this drilldown feature with Highcharts and pie charts.

Line Charts

The line chart is also known as a line plot, line graph, or curve chart. It's a type of diagram that displays information in a series of data points, which are called markers. These markers connect by straight lines. Let's create a simple line chart. See Listing 4-7.

Listing 4-7. Linechart.component.ts

```
import { Component, OnInit } from '@angular/core';
import * as Highcharts from "highcharts";

@Component({
  selector: 'app-line-chart',
  templateUrl: './line-chart.component.html',
```

```
  styleUrls: ['./line-chart.component.css']
})
export class LineChartComponent {
  title = 'myHighChartsApp';
  highcharts = Highcharts;
  chartOptions: Highcharts.Options = {
    chart: {
      type: 'line'
    },
    title: {
      text: 'Industry Growth by Sector, 2017-2022'
    },
  xAxis: {
  categories: ["2017", "2018", "2019", "2020", "2021", "2022"]
    },
    yAxis: {
      title: {
        text: 'Revenue Generated in million'
      }
    },
    legend: {
      layout: 'vertical',
      align: 'right',
      verticalAlign: 'middle'
    },
    series: [{
      type:'line',
      name: 'IT',
      data: [400, 489, 354, 180, 785, 293]
    }, {
      type:'line',
      name: 'Cement',
      data: [180, 100, 50, 89, 105, 206]
    }, {
      type:'line',
```

```
    name: 'Pharmacy',
    data: [350, 400, 250, 400, 550, 480]
  }, {
    type:'line',
    name: 'Agriculture',
    data: [190, 210, 250, 280, 310, 500]
  }],
  }
}
```

This code is basic line chart code where you create a chart to see industry growth with multiple lines. By default, in Highcharts, the chart type is set as line. If you do not assign a chart type, it will draw a line chart for you. See Figure 4-8.

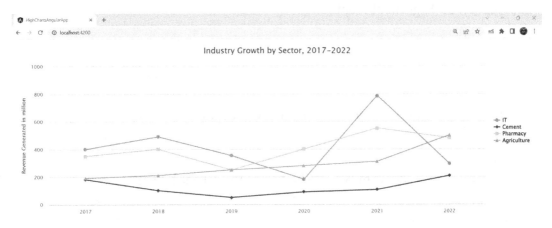

Figure 4-8. *Basic multiple line chart*

Area Charts

An area chart represents changes that happen over time; it used to display quantitative data. At the time of development, the Highcharts chart type is area. In this chart, the x-axis part is shaded with colors. Let's create your first area chart. Copy Listing 4-8 into the areachart.component.ts file.

Listing 4-8. areachart.component.ts

```typescript
import { Component } from '@angular/core';
import * as Highcharts from 'highcharts';

@Component({
  selector: 'app-areachart',
  templateUrl: './areachart.component.html',
  styleUrls: ['./areachart.component.css']
})

export class AreachartComponent {
  title = 'myHighChartsApp';
  Highcharts: typeof Highcharts = Highcharts;
  chartOptions: Highcharts.Options = {
    chart: {
      type: 'area'
    },
    title: {
      text: 'Average scored by students in Computer Science'
    },
    xAxis: {
      categories: ['Quarterly', 'Six Monthly', 'Final Year'],
    },
    yAxis: {
      title: {
        text: 'Average Scores'
      }
    },
    legend: {
      layout: 'vertical',
      align: 'right',
      verticalAlign: 'middle'
    },
    series: [{
      type:'area',
      name: 'Science Score',
```

```
      data: [45, 75, 80]
    }],
  }
}
```

This is just a simple area chart to help you understand how to develop an area chart with Highcharts. Once you run this code, you will get output like Figure 4-9.

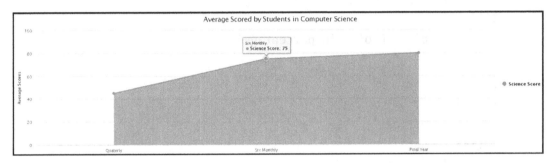

Figure 4-9. *Basic area chart*

Listing 4-9 shows how to develop an area chart with negative values.

Listing 4-9. areachart.component.ts

```typescript
import { Component, OnInit } from '@angular/core';
import * as Highcharts from 'highcharts';

@Component({
  selector: 'app-areachart',
  templateUrl: './areachart.component.html',
  styleUrls: ['./areachart.component.css']
})
export class AreachartComponent {
 title = 'myHighChartsApp';
  Highcharts: typeof Highcharts = Highcharts;
  chartOptions: Highcharts.Options = {
    chart: {
      type: 'area'
    },
```

```
    title: {
       text: 'Yearly Performance of XYZ Mutual Fund'
       },
       xAxis: {
       categories: ["2018","2019", "2020", "2021","2022"],
       },
       yAxis: {
       title: {
       text: 'Absolute Profit in percentage'
       }
       },
       legend: {
       layout: 'vertical',
       align: 'right',
       verticalAlign: 'middle'
       },
       series: [{
       name: 'Large Cap',
       type:'area',
       data: [10, 8, 12, 15, -2]
       }, {
       name: 'Mid cap',
       type:'area',
       data: [9, 6.5, 7, 18, 5]
       }, {
       name: 'Small cap',
       type:'area',
       data: [5.6, -2, -3, 25, 3]
       }],
 }
}
```

As you can see in Listing 4-9, in different series there are negative values based on the area chart constructed (Figure 4-10).

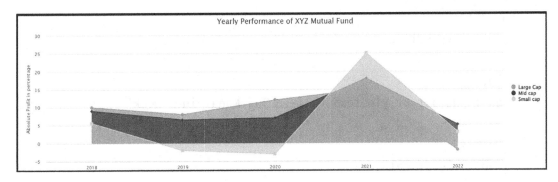

Figure 4-10. *Area chart with negative values*

In the next example, you will learn about the area-spline chart, which has features of the area and spline charts. Let's take a look. Copy the complete code in Listing 4-10 into the areachart.`component.ts` file.

Listing 4-10. areachart.component.ts

```
import { Component, OnInit } from '@angular/core';
import * as Highcharts from 'highcharts';

@Component({
  selector: 'app-areachart',
  templateUrl: './areachart.component.html',
  styleUrls: ['./areachart.component.css']
})

}
import { Component, OnInit } from '@angular/core';
import * as Highcharts from 'highcharts';

@Component({
  selector: 'app-area-spline-chart',
  templateUrl: './area-spline-chart.component.html',
  styleUrls: ['./area-spline-chart.component.css']
})
export class AreaSplineChartComponent {
  title = 'myHighChartsApp';
  Highcharts: typeof Highcharts = Highcharts;
  chartOptions: Highcharts.Options = {
```

61

```
chart: {
  type: 'areaspline'
},
title: {
  text: 'Number of visitors visited Taj Mahal in a week'
},
legend: {
  layout: 'vertical',
  align: 'left',
  verticalAlign: 'top',
},
xAxis: {
  categories: [
    'Monday',
    'Tuesday',
    'Wednesday',
    'Thursday',
    'Friday',
    'Saturday',
    'Sunday'
  ],
  plotBands: [{ // Design to visualize the weekend
    from: 5,
    to: 6,
    color: 'orange'
  }]
},
yAxis: {
  title: {
    text: 'Number of visitors'
  }
},
tooltip: {
  valueSuffix: ' people'
},
```

```
    plotOptions: {
      areaspline: {
        fillOpacity: 0.6
      }
    },
    series: [{
      type: 'areaspline',
      name: 'Taj Mahal',
      data: [5000, 2700, 3200, 3800, 4100, 5600, 6000]
    }]
  };
}
```

Listing 4-10 is the example of an area-spline chart, which is the combination of area and spline charts. This chart demonstrates how many visitors come to see the Taj Mahal in a week. If you set the code chart `type` as `areaspline`, you can use the `plotBands` property to highlight the weekend in the chart (Figure 4-11):

```
plotBands: [{ // Design to visualize the weekend
    from:5,
    to: 6,
    color: 'orange'
}]
```

Here you use two properties, `from` and `to`, so `from` demonstrates where to start and `to` describes where to end. The count starts from 0. You want to start on Saturday, so you set 5 as the `from` property and 6 as the `to` property. See Figure 4-11.

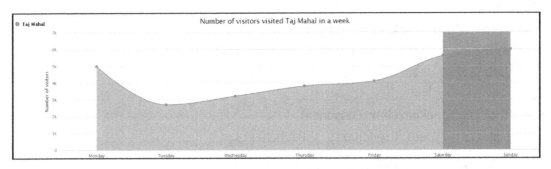

Figure 4-11. *Area-spline chart with plotBands*

Scatter Charts

A scatter plot, also known as a scatter graph, scattergram, or scatter chart, is a type of plot that uses Cartesian coordinates to display typically two variables for a set of data. Points are coded and defined using color and shape/size. Data is presented in the collection of points; each point has one value. Copy the code in Listing 4-11 into `stacked bar-chart.component.ts`.

Listing 4-11. stacked bar-chart.component.ts

```
import { Component, OnInit } from '@angular/core';
import * as Highcharts from 'highcharts';

// Extend SeriesStatesHoverOptionsObject type
interface ExtendedSeriesStatesHoverOptionsObject
  extends Highcharts.SeriesStatesHoverOptionsObject {
  marker: object;
}

// Extend XAxisTitleOptions type
interface ExtendedXAxisTitleOptions extends Highcharts.XAxisTitleOptions {
  enabled: boolean;
}

interface ExtenedZoom extends Highcharts.ChartOptions
{
  zoomType: string
}

@Component({
  selector: 'app-stackbar-chart',
  templateUrl: './stackbar-chart.component.html',
  styleUrls: ['./stackbar-chart.component.css']
})
export class StackbarChartComponent {
  Highcharts: typeof Highcharts = Highcharts;

  chartOptions: Highcharts.Options = {
    chart: {
```

```
  type: 'scatter',
  zoomType: 'xy',
} as ExtenedZoom,
title: {
  text: 'Height V/s Weight of S.T. Thomas Collage by Gender',
},
xAxis: {
  title: {
    enabled: true,
    text: 'Height (cm)',
  } as ExtendedXAxisTitleOptions,
  startOnTick: true,
  endOnTick: true,
  showLastLabel: true,
},
yAxis: {
  title: {
    text: 'Weight (kg)',
  },
},
legend: {
  layout: 'vertical',
  align: 'left',
  verticalAlign: 'top',
  x: 150,
  y: 40,
  floating: true,
  borderWidth: 1,
},
plotOptions: {
  scatter: {
    marker: {
      radius: 5,
      states: {
        hover: {
```

```
              enabled: true,
              lineColor: 'black',
            },
          },
        },
        states: {
          hover: {
            marker: {
              enabled: false,
            },
          } as ExtendedSeriesStatesHoverOptionsObject,
        },
        tooltip: {
          headerFormat: '<b>{series.name}</b><br>',
          pointFormat: '{point.x} cm, {point.y} kg',
        },
      },
    },
    series: [
      {
        type: 'scatter',
        name: 'Female',
        color: 'red',
        data: [
          [151.2, 53.1],
          [157.3, 51.0],
          [169.5, 69.2],
          [147.0, 50.0],
          [175.8, 83.6],
          [150.0, 51.0],
          [151.1, 57.9],
          [156.0, 79.8],
          [146.2, 46.8],
          [158.1, 74.9]
        ],
```

```
      },
      {
        type: 'scatter',
        name: 'Male',
        color: 'blue',
        data: [
          [172.0, 63.7],
          [165.3, 72.7],
          [183.5, 79.2],
          [176.5, 75.7],
          [177.2, 85.8],
          [171.5, 64.8],
          [181, 82.4],
          [174.5, 77.4],
          [177.0, 61.0],
          [174.0, 83.7]
        ],
      },
    ],
  };
}
```

Listing 4-11 gives you a chart of the height and weight of students based on their gender.

Before explaining this code, you must understand the TypeScript extending interface. TypeScript allows an interface to extend a class; with this extend keyword the interface inherits properties and methods. In Highcharts, sometimes you must use inheritance features to extend your classes. In Listing 4-11, you use extend three times. Let's explore the ExtendedZoom interface:

interface ExtendedZoom extends Highcharts.ChartOptions

```
{
    zoomType: string
}
```

In Highcharts, there is a property called zoomType is xy, and it means if you drag your mouse on the x-axis or y-axis, your graph will automatically zoom. The zoomType property can be used in any graph in the chart section. For this property, you must extend Highcharts.ChartOptions and then define its property zoomType as string.

The code chart type is scatter:

```
chart: {
        type: 'scatter',
        zoomType: 'xy',
    } as ExtenedZoom,
```

In the plotOptions section, you can set the scatter subproperty as the radius of a circle for line color once a mouse hovers.

```
plotOptions: {
    scatter: {
      marker: {
        radius: 5,
        states: {
          hover: {
            enabled: true,
            lineColor: 'black'
          }
        }
      },
      states: {
          hover: {
            marker: {
              enabled: false,
            },
          } as ExtendedSeriesStatesHoverOptionsObject,
      },
      tooltip: {
        headerFormat: '<b>{series.name}</b><br>',
        pointFormat: '{point.x} cm, {point.y} kg'
```

```
      }
    }
  }
```

Run this code and you will get the output shown in Figure 4-12.

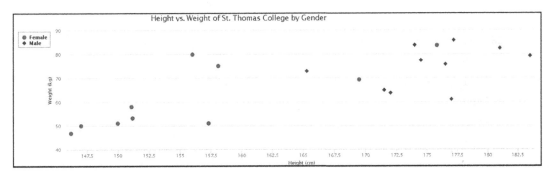

Figure 4-12. *Scatter chart*

Histogram Charts

A histogram chart is the way to put a group of data into a user-specified range. A histogram looks like a bar chart. This type of chart is used for statistical analysis to illustrate how many kinds of variables are in a specific range, such as data in the form of graph, like census data of a state or how many people are a particular age. See Listing 4-12.

Listing 4-12. histogram.component.ts

```
import { Component } from '@angular/core';
import * as Highcharts from 'highcharts';
@Component({
selector: 'app-root',
templateUrl: './app.component.html',
styleUrls: ['./app.component.css']
})
export class AppComponent {
  title = 'myHighChartsApp';
Highcharts: typeof Highcharts = Highcharts;
  chartOptions: Highcharts.Options = {
    chart: {
```

```
      type: 'column'
   },
   title: {
     text: 'Histogram for Rainfall'
   },
   xAxis: {
     categories: [
       'Jun',
       'Jul',
       'Aug',
       'Sep',
       'Oct',
     ],
     crosshair: true
   },
   yAxis: {
     title: { text: 'Rain in mm' },
     min: 0,
   },
   plotOptions: {
     column: {
       pointPadding: 0,
       borderWidth: 0,
       groupPadding: 0,
       shadow: false
     }
   },
   series: [{
     type: 'column',
     name: 'Month',
     data: [49.9, 71.5, 106.4, 129.2, 144.0]
   }]
 };
}
```

This histogram chart is developed by setting the chart type to column. For this, you set plotOptions as

```
plotOptions: {
    column: {
      pointPadding: 0,
      borderWidth: 0,
      groupPadding: 0,
      shadow: false
    }
  },
```

Once you run this chart, you will get the result shown in Figure 4-13.

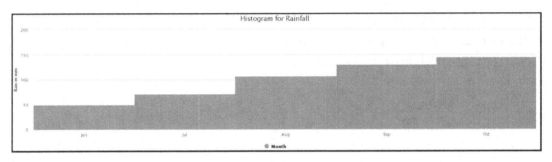

Figure 4-13. *Basic histogram chart with chart type as column*

Heat Map Series Charts

A heat map series chart is the way to represent data values in the form of a matrix. The matrix is defined by different colors. If you want to implement a heat map series for your dashboard, you have to configure the following things:

jQuery: Add this code to the script section:

```
<script src="https://code.highcharts.com/modules/heatmap.js"></script>
```

Angular: Add this code to the app.component.ts file:

```
import Heatmap from 'highcharts/modules/heatmap';
Heatmap(Highcharts);
```

Now see Listing 4-13.

Listing 4-13. heatmap-series-chart.component.ts

```typescript
import { Component, OnInit } from '@angular/core';
import * as Highcharts from 'highcharts';
import Heatmap from 'highcharts/modules/heatmap';
Heatmap(Highcharts);

@Component({
  selector: 'app-heatmap-series-chart',
  templateUrl: './heatmap-series-chart.component.html',
  styleUrls: ['./heatmap-series-chart.component.css']
})
export class HeatmapSeriesChartComponent {

  title = 'myHighChartsApp';
  Highcharts: typeof Highcharts = Highcharts;
  chartOptions: Highcharts.Options = {
    chart: {
      type: 'heatmap',
      plotBorderWidth: 1
    },
    title: {
      text: 'Daily marks obtained per student per weekday'
    },
    xAxis: {
      categories: ['John', 'Dale', 'Jacob', 'Johnson', 'Thomas', 'James',
      'Mike', 'Jaeffry', 'Ben', 'Jack']
    },
    yAxis: {
      categories: ['Monday', 'Tuesday', 'Wednesday', 'Thursday', 'Friday'],
    },
    colorAxis: {
      min: 0,
      minColor: '#FFFFFF',
      maxColor: "#ADD8E6",
    },
```

```
    legend: {
      align: 'right',
      layout: 'vertical',
      margin: 0,
      verticalAlign: 'top',
      y: 25,
      symbolHeight: 280
    },
    series: [{
      type: 'heatmap',
      name: 'Marks per student',
      borderWidth: 1,
      data: [[0, 0, 10], [0, 1, 19], [0, 2, 8], [0, 3, 24], [0, 4, 67], [1,
      0, 92], [1, 1, 58], [1, 2, 78], [1, 3, 94], [1, 4, 48], [2, 0, 35],
      [2, 1, 15], [2, 2, 84], [2, 3, 64], [2, 4, 52], [3, 0, 72], [3, 1,
      78], [3, 2, 98], [3, 3, 19], [3, 4, 16], [4, 0, 38], [4, 1, 5], [4,
      2, 8], [4, 3, 75], [4, 4, 55], [5, 0, 88], [5, 1, 32], [5, 2, 12],
      [5, 3, 6], [5, 4, 50], [6, 0, 13], [6, 1, 44], [6, 2, 88], [6, 3,
      98], [6, 4, 96], [7, 0, 31], [7, 1, 1], [7, 2, 82], [7, 3, 32], [7,
      4, 30], [8, 0, 85], [8, 1, 97], [8, 2, 123], [8, 3, 64], [8, 4, 84],
      [9, 0, 47], [9, 1, 24], [9, 2, 31], [9, 3, 48], [9, 4, 91]],
      dataLabels: {
        enabled: true,
        color: '#000000'
      }
    }]
  }
}
```

In Listing 4-13, the chart type is heatmap. This example shows the marks of different students over the course of a week, in the form of a matrix. The x-axis shows student names. If you run this code, you will get the output in Figure 4-14.

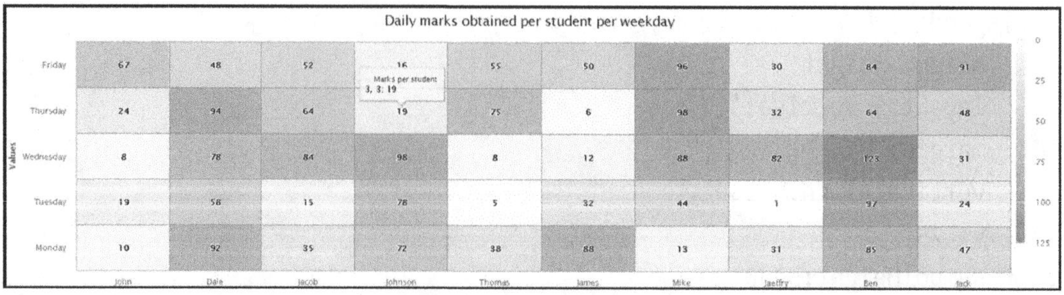

Figure 4-14. *Heat map series chart*

As you can see, the right-hand side legend is a different kind of legend. This kind of legend is provided in a heatmap. See the following code:

```
legend: {
    align: 'right',
    layout: 'vertical',
    margin: 0,
    verticalAlign: 'top',
    y: 25,
    symbolHeight: 280
},
```

In the series section, data is written like data:[[0,0,10],[0,1,19]...], so here it's defined in the form of the column, row, and marks. This is the way to define a matrix.

Stacked Bar Charts

A stacked chart represents different groups on top of each other. The height of the bar represents the combined result of the group. Stacked bars are not suitable when some groups have negative values. Let's take a look. See Listing 4-14.

Listing 4-14. stackbar-chart.component.ts

```
import { Component, OnInit } from '@angular/core';
import * as Highcharts from 'highcharts';

@Component({
  selector: 'app-stackbar-chart',
```

```
  templateUrl: './stackbar-chart.component.html',
  styleUrls: ['./stackbar-chart.component.css']
})
export class StackbarChartComponent {
  title = 'myHighChartsApp';
  Highcharts: typeof Highcharts = Highcharts;
  chartOptions: Highcharts.Options = {
    chart: {
      type: 'column'
    },
    title: {
      text: 'Total hours studies in a week'
    },
    xAxis: {
      categories: ['Maths', 'Science', 'History', 'Social Science',
      'English']
    },
    yAxis: {
      min: 0,
      title: {
        text: 'Total Hour studied'
      },
      stackLabels: {
        enabled: true,
        style: {
          color: 'gray'
        }
      }
    },
    legend: {
      align: 'right',
      x: -30,
      verticalAlign: 'top',
      y: 25,
      floating: true,
      backgroundColor:
```

```
          'yellow' || 'white',
      borderColor: '#CCC',
      borderWidth: 1,
      shadow: false
    },
    plotOptions: {
      column: {
        stacking: 'normal',
        dataLabels: {
          enabled: true
        }
      }
    },
    series: [{
      type: 'column',
      name: 'Rocy',
      data: [4, 2, 1, 8, 9]
    },
    {
      name: 'Luies',
      type: 'column',
      data: [1, 5, 1, 4, 2]
    },
    {
      type: 'column',
      name: 'Simon',
      data: [7, 2, 3, 1, 4]
    }]
  }
}
```

This code is a perfect example of a stacked chart. This code calculates the total hours a student spends on a particular subject in a week. The chart type is column; in Highcharts, there is no stackedchart type, but you can develop one with a bar column very quickly if you set the plotOptions subproperty as stacking: 'normal'. This means this property is responsible for stacking each series on top of each other.

```
plotOptions: {
    column: {
      stacking: 'normal',
      dataLabels: {enabled: true }
    }
}
```

For better understating, add labels into each series group. For this, see the following code. In y-axis, you use the stackLabels property, and then the subproperty, which is

```
yAxis: {
    min: 0,
    title: {
      text: 'Total Hour studied'
    },
    stackLabels: {
      enabled: true,
      style: {
        color: 'gray'
      }
    }
  }
```

Set enabled: true so the labels are in each series. Then add some styling for the text of the labels. Figure 4-15 shows the output of Listing 4-14.

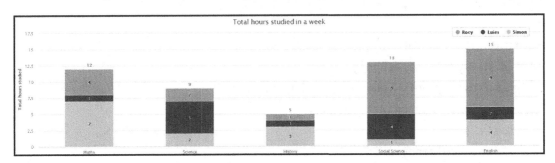

Figure 4-15. *Stacked bar chart with columns*

Column Pyramid Charts

A column pyramid chart is a kind of column chart, only it looks like a pyramid. Pyramid charts are designed for comparing data with discrete data with values instead of categories.

To develop a simple pyramid chart, these dependencies are required:

For jQuery users:

```
<script src="https://code.highcharts.com/highcharts-more.js"></script>
```

For Angular users:

```
import More from 'highcharts/highcharts-more';
More(Highcharts);
```

Now let's create a pyramid chart. See Listing 4-15.

Listing 4-15. pyramid-chart.component.ts

```
import { Component, OnInit } from '@angular/core';
import * as Highcharts from 'highcharts';
import More from 'highcharts/highcharts-more';
More(Highcharts);
@Component({
  selector: 'app-pyramid-chart',
  templateUrl: './pyramid-chart.component.html',
  styleUrls: ['./pyramid-chart.component.css']
})
export class PyramidChartComponent {
  title = 'myHighChartsApp';
  Highcharts: typeof Highcharts = Highcharts;
  chartOptions: Highcharts.Options = {
    chart: {
      type: 'columnpyramid'
    },
    title: {
      text: 'Height of different students in a class'
    },
```

```
  colors: ['red', 'blue', 'green', 'yellow', 'pink'],
  xAxis: {
    type: 'category',
    crosshair: true,
    labels: {
      style: {
        fontSize: '10px'
      }
    },
  },
  yAxis: {
    min: 0,
    title: {
      text: 'Height (cm)'
    }
  },
  tooltip: {
    valueSuffix: ' cm'
  },
  series: [{
    name: 'Height',
    type: 'columnpyramid',
    colorByPoint: true,
    showInLegend: true,
    data: [
      ['Mohan', 162.56],
      ['Ram', 177.8],
      ['John', 157.48],
      ['Daisy', 160],
      ['Mike', 175.5]
    ],
  }]
};
}
```

In this code, the chart type is columnpyramid. This code creates a series of students' heights. In this code, as you can see, all pyramids are in a different color.

For this, in the series section, a subproperty is

colorByPoint: true

If you set this property as false, all series pyramids will be the same color. Now type ng serve and you will get output shown in Figure 4-16.

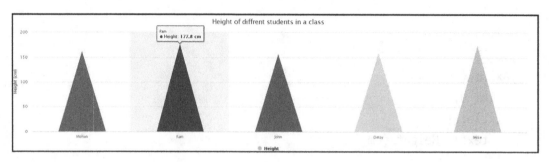

Figure 4-16. *Simple column pyramid chart*

You can also develop a stacked column pyramid chart very quickly using Highcharts. Listing 4-16 calculates the total hours spent by a student in a week on a particular subject.

Listing 4-16. stack-pyramid-chart.component.ts

```
import { Component, OnInit } from '@angular/core';
import * as Highcharts from 'highcharts';
import More from 'highcharts/highcharts-more';
More(Highcharts);

@Component({
  selector: 'app-stack-pyramid-chart',
  templateUrl: './stack-pyramid-chart.component.html',
  styleUrls: ['./stack-pyramid-chart.component.css']
})
export class StackPyramidChartComponent {
  title = 'myHighChartsApp';
  Highcharts: typeof Highcharts = Highcharts;
  chartOptions: Highcharts.Options = {
    chart: {
```

```
    type: 'columnpyramid'
  },
  title: {
    text: 'Stacked columnpyramid chart'
  },
  xAxis: {
categories: ['Maths', 'Science', 'History', 'Social Science', 'English']
  },
  yAxis: {
    min: 0,
    title: {
      text: 'Total Hour studied'
    },
    stackLabels: {
      enabled: true,
      style: {
        fontWeight: 'bold',
        color: 'gray'
      }
    }
  },
  legend: {
    align: 'right',
    x: -30,
    verticalAlign: 'top',
    y: 25,
    floating: true,
    backgroundColor: 'white',
    borderColor: '#CCC',
    borderWidth: 1,
    shadow: false
  },
  tooltip: {
    headerFormat: '<b>{point.x}</b><br/>',
    pointFormat: '{series.name}: {point.y}<br/>Total: {point.stackTotal}'
```

```
    },
    plotOptions: {
      columnpyramid: {
        stacking: 'normal',
        dataLabels: {
          enabled: true,
          color: 'white'
        }
      }
    },
    series: [{
      type: 'columnpyramid',
      name: 'Rocy',
      data: [4, 2, 1, 8, 9]
    }, { type: 'columnpyramid', name: 'Luies', data: [1, 5, 1, 4, 2] },
    {
      type: 'columnpyramid', name: 'Simon', data: [7, 2, 3, 1, 4]
    }]
  }
}
```

In Listing 4-16, the chart `type` is `columnpyramid`, but in `plotOptions`, note that `stacking: 'normal'`. This property helps create a stacked based chart in Highcharts.

```
  plotOptions: {
    columnpyramid: {
      stacking: 'normal',
      dataLabels: {
        enabled: true,
        color: 'white'
      }
    }
  },
```

If you run the code, you will get Figure 4-17.

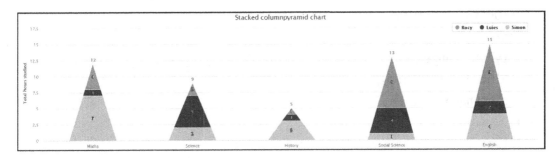

Figure 4-17. *Stacked column pyramid chart*

Gauge Charts

A gauge chart is also known as a dial chart or a speedometer chart. This type of chart reads the needle on the dial and can provide great visualization for a dashboard. Gauge charts are mostly used by aircraft pilots. Let's take a look at how you can implement a gauge chart using Highcharts and Angular. See Listing 4-17.

Listing 4-17. gauge-chart.component.ts

```
import { Component } from "@angular/core";
import * as Highcharts from "highcharts";
import More from 'highcharts/highcharts-more';
import solidGauge from "highcharts//modules/solid-gauge.js";

More(Highcharts);
solidGauge(Highcharts);

@Component({
  selector: 'app-gauge-chart',
  templateUrl: './gauge-chart.component.html',
  styleUrls: ['./gauge-chart.component.css']
})
export class GaugeChartComponent {
  title = 'myHighChartsApp';
  Highcharts: typeof Highcharts = Highcharts;
```

```
chartOptions: Highcharts.Options = {
  chart: {
    type: 'gauge',
    plotBorderWidth: 0,
    plotShadow: false
  },
  title: {
    text: 'Speedometer'
  },
  pane: {
    startAngle: -150,
    endAngle: 150,
    background: [{
      backgroundColor: {
        linearGradient: { x1: 0, y1: 0, x2: 0, y2: 1 },
        stops: [
          [0, '#FFF'],
          [1, '#333']
        ]
      },
      borderWidth: 0,
      outerRadius: '109%'
    }, {
      backgroundColor: {
        linearGradient: { x1: 0, y1: 0, x2: 0, y2: 1 },
        stops: [
          [0, '#333'],
          [1, '#FFF']
        ]
      },
      borderWidth: 1,
      outerRadius: '107%'
    }, {
      // default background
    }, {
      backgroundColor: '#DDD',
```

```
      borderWidth: 0,
      outerRadius: '105%',
      innerRadius: '103%'
  }]
},
yAxis : {
  min: 0,
  max: 200,
  minorTickInterval: 'auto',
  minorTickWidth: 1,
  minorTickLength: 10,
  minorTickPosition: 'inside',
  minorTickColor: '#666',
  tickPixelInterval: 30,
  tickWidth: 2,
  tickPosition: 'inside',
  tickLength: 10,
  tickColor: '#666',
  labels: {
    step: 2
  },
  title: {
    text: 'km/h'
  },
  plotBands: [{
    from: 0,
    to: 120,
    color: '#55BF3B' // green
  }, {
    from: 120,
    to: 160,
    color: '#DDDF0D' // yellow
  }, {
    from: 160,
    to: 200,
    color: '#DF5353' // red
```

```
    }]
  },
  plotOptions: {
    solidgauge: {
      dataLabels: {
        y: 5,
        borderWidth: 0,
        useHTML: true
      }
    }
  },
  series: [{
    type: 'gauge',
    name: 'Speed',
    data: [60],
    tooltip: {
      valueSuffix: ' km/h'
    }
  }]
};
}
```

Let's understand Listing 4-17. The chart type is gauge. The pane section is

```
pane: {
    startAngle: -150,
    endAngle: 150,
    background: [{
     backgroundColor: {
      linearGradient: { x1: 0, y1: 0, x2: 0, y2: 1 },
      stops: [
       [0, '#FFF'],
       [1, '#333']
      ]
     },
     borderWidth: 0,
     outerRadius: '109%'
```

```
}, {
 backgroundColor: {
  linearGradient: { x1: 0, y1: 0, x2: 0, y2: 1 },
  stops: [
   [0, '#333'],
   [1, '#FFF']
  ]
 },
 borderWidth: 1,
 outerRadius: '107%'
}, {
 // default background
}, {
 backgroundColor: '#DDD',
 borderWidth: 0,
 outerRadius: '105%',
 innerRadius: '103%'
}]
},
```

In the gauge, the startAngle from the start angle of the x-axis is given in degrees where 0 means north. The endAngle of the x-axis is given in degrees where 0 is north.

The y-axis is where you set the minimum and maximum speed for the gauge:

```
yAxis: {
    min: 0,
    max: 200,
    minorTickInterval: 'auto',
    minorTickWidth: 1,
    minorTickLength: 10,
    minorTickPosition: 'inside',
    minorTickColor: '#666',
    tickPixelInterval: 30,
    tickWidth: 2,
    tickPosition: 'inside',
    tickLength: 10,
    tickColor: '#666',
```

```
labels: {
 step: 2,
 rotation: 'auto'
},
title: {
 text: 'km/h'
},
plotBands: [{
 from: 0,
 to: 120,
 color: '#55BF3B' // green
}, {
 from: 120,
 to: 160,
 color: '#DDDF0D' // yellow
}, {
 from: 160,
 to: 200,
 color: '#DF5353' // red
}]
},
```

Now you set `plotBands` from where to where based on speed and colors. Then you set your `plotOptions`, and then you define the series. In a later chapter, you will see dynamic gauge charts for your dashboard in detail, but for now, see Figure 4-18.

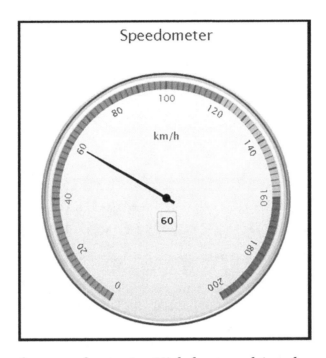

Figure 4-18. *Simple gauge chart using Highcharts and Angular*

Summary

In this chapter, you learned how to easily create different types of charts very quickly with the use of Highcharts. These charts are beneficial for your dashboard based on certain conditions. Some charts required extra dependencies such as stack bars, pyramids, heatmaps, and so on. Based on your JavaScript framework, Angular or jQuery, please add those dependencies first in your project, as mentioned. In the upcoming chapters, you will see more charting types, which will help you make great charts based on your customer requirements.

CHAPTER 5

Working with Real-Time Data

Sourabh Mishra[a*]

   [a] IECE Digital, Bangalore, India

In this chapter, you will learn how to get real-time data from the server side and render it into Highcharts using Angular. To work on real-time data, you must configure and send a request to a backend service (such as a web API, WCF, Web Services, REST Services, etc.), which can fetch data from the server, and the response will provide data for a Highcharts series. This chapter will talk about web APIs and how you can develop a web API using Visual Studio, which will consume this web API into your single page application for rendering real-time data.

Web API

API means *application programming interface*, and a web API is a kind of business logic interface where users can consume and access methods (based on permissions) for specific features. These methods are called *resources*, and these methods are in the layer of HTTP verbs. A web API has four types of common verbs:

- HttpGet
- HttpPost
- HttpPut
- HttpDelete

© Sourabh Mishra 2023

S. Mishra, *Practical Highcharts with Angular*, https://doi.org/10.1007/978-1-4842-9181-8_5

They correspond to

- HttpGet - Read

- HttpPost - Insert (Create)

- HttpPut - Update

- HttpDelete - Delete

Figure 5-1 illustrates this request-response model in web API services.

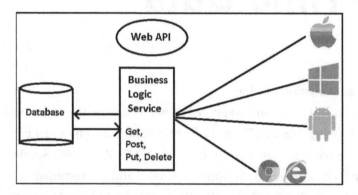

Figure 5-1. *Web API framework*

For example, you write one method to access and share live market data, and you host your service. Now, if a different application wants to access your service for fetching data, it will consume that particular web API, the one accessed by the HTTP protocol. As the name suggests, a web API works over the Web. A web API is an excellent framework because it reaches many clients; they can be accessed/consumed through browsers, IoT applications, and mobile devices very quickly.

Figure 5-1 shows three sections:

- Database

- Web API

- Browser and devices

The request comes from the browser or mobile app to the web API services. In a web API, all methods and business logic are written. If a requested resource is permitted to access a method, in the next step it will go to the database and fetch information, and the response will be returned in the form of XML or JSON based on your return type.

What Is REST?

Rest stands for *representational states transfer*, and it is an architectural pattern. Roy Fielding first introduced REST in 2000 in his doctoral presentation. In REST, communication is always stateless. Here *stateless* means if you send one request, after getting a response, the relationship will break, so you must send a new request and get a new response. If you want to maintain your state, you can keep it on the client side. In REST, you can define multiple responses for the same resource method, so you can get a response in the form of JSON, XML, CSV, JPG, PDF, HTML, and more. REST uses the HTTP methods to operate resources in the form of get, put, post, and delete.

The following is an example of the JSON format and it comes from a response:

```
{"studentId":1,"studentName":"ram","phone":982641***,"address":"delhi"}
```

Here each resource/method has one unique identifier, which will send a request to access a method and get the responses. For example,

- Get: https://localhost:5001/api/getStudents/

- Post: https://localhost:5001/api/AddStudent/

- Put: https://localhost:5001/api/UpdateStudent/

- Delete: https://localhost:5001/api/DeleteStudent/

Now let's build a project with Angular and a web API using Highcharts.

Web API Development Using Visual Studio

This application is pretty simple. You'll create a line chart based on student performance in particular subjects. For this application, you have two different apps.

For the server side, you will write one web API service with a SQL Server database using Entity Framework. For the other side, you will use the Angular application you developed in Chapter 3. In this chapter, you will just enhance this application with a web API.

To create the web API application, open Visual Studio and go to File ➤ New ➤ Project ➤ Select Asp.Net Core Web Application (Figure 5-2).

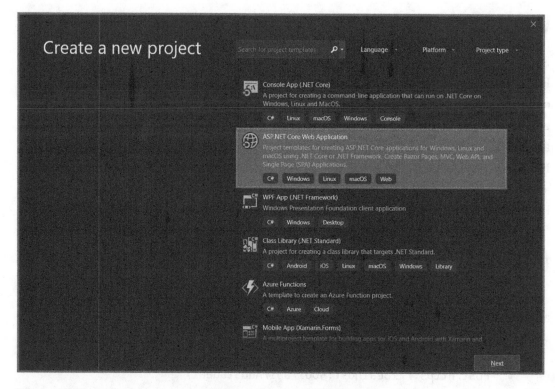

Figure 5-2. *Creating a new web API using Visual Studio*

Click the Next button. You will get the screen shown in Figure 5-3.

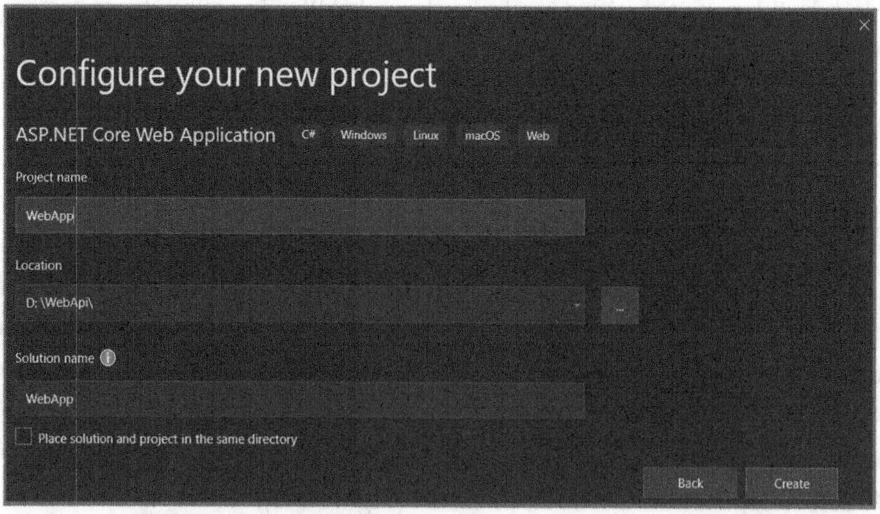

Figure 5-3. *Configuring a new project*

Here you can set the project name and location path (which particular directory you want to save in) of your project. After you fill in these fields, click the Create button.

Next, you'll create a web API project (Figure 5-4), so choose an API and click the Create button. Your new web API will be created. Once your API has been created, you will see all related files and folders in Solution Explorer. Let's understand Solution Explorer and what files and folders come with the new web API project.

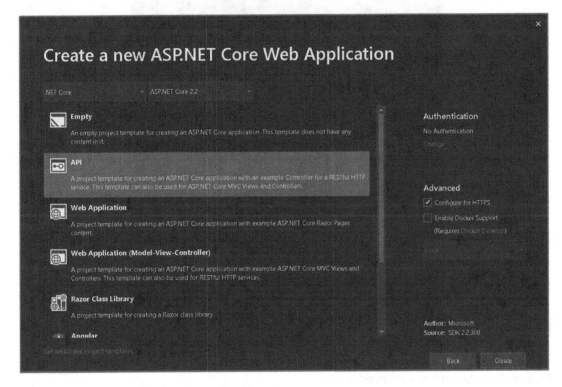

Figure 5-4. *Project template selection screen*

Solution Explorer

In Visual Studio, Solution Explorer is the place where you see your project file structure. In one solution, you can see more than one project. Here you can add/remove files or projects and include/exclude files for your project.

Figure 5-5 shows Solution Explorer. If you are not able to see this in your Visual Studio, go to View ➤ Solution Explorer, and you will get the info shown in Figure 5-5.

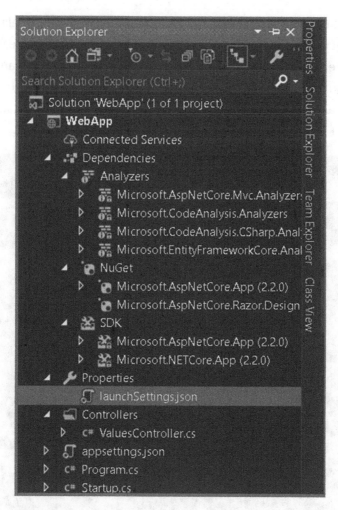

Figure 5-5. *Solution Explorer*

Let's explore all the required files and folders one by one.

- **Dependencies**: This folder is designed for all project-related dependencies, such as NuGet-related packages, project analyzer-related packages, and SDK-related packages. As per your requirements, you can add more dependencies here.

- **Properties**: This folder contains the launchSettings.json file. In this file, you can set project launch-related settings, which means when you press F5 to run your project, which particular API you want to run, you can place an environment variable.

- **Controller**: This is the most important folder for a web API because you add all API controllers here and it's where you write your methods and business logic.

- **appSettings.json**: All application-related settings are set here.

- **Program.cs**: All ASP.NET core-based projects are ignited from the console application. **Program.cs** is the execution point; you can see here the **Main** method. This method is connected with **startup.cs** and is required to run the app.

- **Startup.cs**: This file is responsible for all the configuration methods for the project. The following sections describe the required methods.

ConfigureService( )

You can find the **ConfigureService()** method in **Startup.cs**. It's where you set all dependency injection-related kinds of stuff. Note that the .NET core comes with a built-in IOC container concept. Now no third party containers are required.

But what is dependency injection? In an object-oriented programming world, you create classes, and whenever you want to use these classes, you create objects. For example, you have a class called **Maths**:

```
public class Maths
{
public int Add(int a,int b)
{
int c=a+b;
}
}
```

For this **Maths** class, if you want to access its methods, you must create an object of the **Maths** class in this way:

```
var obj = new Maths();
```

If you want to access this object method, you must call it like

```
obj.Add(12,3);
```

It is related to the object creation thing. If you don't want to create objects in this way, you go for IOC (inversion of control). When you want to invert object creational stuff to someone else, it's called the IOC pattern, and dependency injection is the way to implement IOC.

With the use of dependency injection, you don't need to create objects all the time. This gets taken care of automatically. One way of implementing dependency injection is to inject your object into the constructor level. In the upcoming chapters, you will explore this concept more.

Configure( )

Configure() is one more method you can find in Startup.cs. In this method, you can set your application request pipeline, which means what comes first and what comes next. The .NET core is designed to make your application lightweight so you only call the required dependencies and requests here.

Routing

In the browser, whenever you want to open a site, you need a URL. Every URL has a path, like www.apress.com/in/about. In this URL, /in/about is the address of a particular page. This is helpful for SEO (search engine optimization) purposes also. Here you don't require a map to a file, so routing is a concept where you send the request to a particular URL route. It will render a result in the form of a response.

Attribute Routing

In the ASP.NET web API, you can do attribute routing very easily. This allows you to handle the exact route the user requested. If you open ValuesController.cs, you can see code like this:

```
[Route("api/[controller]")]
```

Here the Route class is decorating the way for the values controller, which means whenever you want to use the controller in your app, you have to call an API/controller name and then the method name and so on. You can also define this:

```
[Route("api/values")]
```

Now open ValuesController.cs, as shown in Listing 5-1.

Listing 5-1. ValuesController.cs

```
using System;
using System.Collections.Generic;
using System.Linq;
using System.Threading.Tasks;
using Microsoft.AspNetCore.Mvc;
namespace WebApp.Controllers
{
[Route("api/[controller]")]
[ApiController]
public class ValuesController : ControllerBase
{
// GET api/values
[HttpGet]
public ActionResult<IEnumerable<string>> Get()
    {
return new string[] { "value1", "value2" };
    }
// GET api/values/5
[HttpGet("{id}")]
public ActionResult<string> Get(int id)
    {
return "value";
    }
// POST api/values
```

```
[HttpPost]
public void Post([FromBody] string value)
    {
    }
// PUT api/values/5
[HttpPut("{id}")]
public void Put(int id, [FromBody] string value)
    {
    }
// DELETE api/values/5
[HttpDelete("{id}")]
public void Delete(int id)
    {
    }
}
}
```

To understand the ValuesController.cs file in more detail, see the following list:

- ControllerBase: This is the base class for a controller without view support. ControllerBase provides many methods that are very useful for handling HTTP requests.

- ApiController: Controllers decorated with this attribute are configured with features and behavior targeted at improving the developer experience for building APIs. When decorated on an assembly, all controllers in the assembly will be treated as controllers with API behavior.

- ActionResult: ActionResult was introduced in ASP.NET core 2.1; it is the return type of the API controller actions. With the use of ActionResult<type>, you can return the kind of value defined in your method.

ActionResult works based on HTTP methods. The following are the list of methods used in a web API:

- HttpGet: Used to retrieve data. A successful get method returns 200 as status code (OK).

- HttpPost: Used for inserting/creating records. The Post method creates new resources and returns a status code of 201. If there is no result, it gives a status code of 204 (No Content). If there are any errors or a client request sends the wrong data, it will return a status code of 400, which is for a bad request.

- HttpPut: Used for updating records. It returns 201 as a status code. Here 204 means no content in the output. 409 status codes are for a conflict.

- HttpDelete: Used for deleting the record. If the deletion is successful, it will return a status code of 204. If the resource does not exist, it will return a status code of 404 (Not Found).

Now it's time to create a new web API controller. Open Solution Explorer. Right-click in the Controller folder ➤ Add ➤ Controller (Figure 5-6).

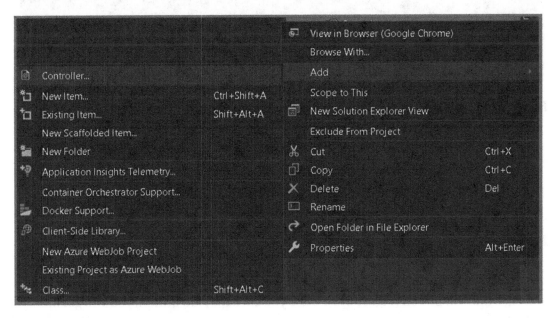

Figure 5-6. *Adding a new controller*

Select API Controller ➤ Empty and click the Add button (Figure 5-7). You will get the screen in Figure 5-8.

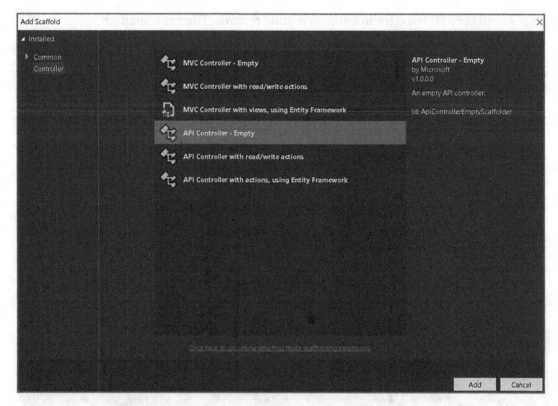

Figure 5-7. *Adding a new API controller*

Figure 5-8. *Adding an empty API controller*

Now it's time to give your controller a name. For this demo, use StudentController, and click the Add button (Figure 5-8). Once you click the Add button, you will get the code shown in Listing 5-2.

Listing 5-2. StudentController.cs

```
using System;
using System.Collections.Generic;
using System.Linq;
```

```
using System.Threading.Tasks;
using Microsoft.AspNetCore.Http;
using Microsoft.AspNetCore.Mvc;
namespace WebApp.Controllers
{
 [Route("api/[controller]")]
 [ApiController]
public class StudentController : ControllerBase
    {
    }
}
```

Now, it's time to work on database activity because you are going to create real-time data, fetch this data, and render it into Highcharts.

Database Creation

If you already have a database and tables, you can skip this section. For database creation, choose your database program as per your requirements, such as SQL Server, Oracle, or MySQL. The only thing you have to remember is the database server name for connecting and the database name.

In this chapter, I will use SQL Server, which comes with Visual Studio.

If you want to continue, go to View ➤ Open SQL Server Object Explorer (Figure 5-9).

1. Open Local Db.

Figure 5-9. *SQL Server Object Explorer*

2. Right-click Databases and select Add New Database.

3. Set the database path and name and then click the OK button (Figure 5-10).

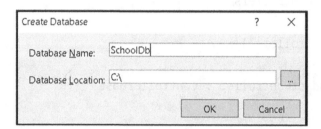

Figure 5-10. *The Create Database screen (for setting the database name and path)*

4. You can see your database on the list. Open it. It will be empty, so let's create a new table.

5. To create a new table, right-click in front of the folder of tables. Add new tables (Figure 5-11).

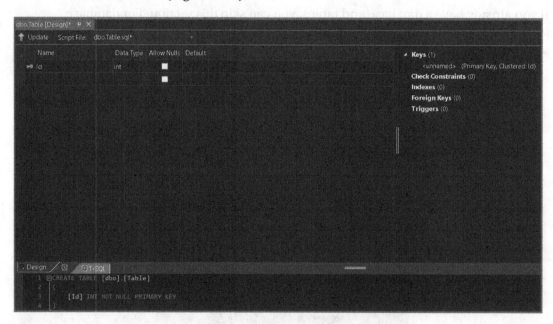

Figure 5-11. *Creating a table through code*

6. Paste the following code and click the Update button:

```
CREATE TABLE [dbo].[StudentMarks](
    [Id]              INTIDENTITY (1, 1)NOT NULL,
    [Name]            NVARCHAR (50) NULL,
    [English]         INT NULL,
    [Maths]           INT NULL,
    [Science]         INT NULL,
PRIMARY KEY CLUSTERED ([Id] ASC)
);
```

7. Once you click the Update button, you will see a new table called StudentMarks.

8. Now it's time to add some data. Right-click in front of the newly created table and choose View Data (Figure 5-12).

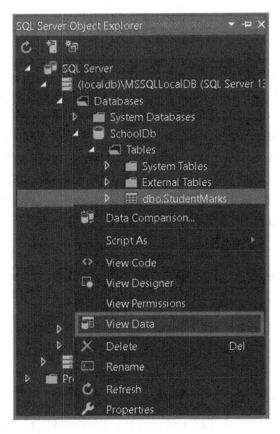

Figure 5-12. *Adding a record process into a table*

9. Now you will get a row- and column-based screen to add records, so add your data in the form of rows and columns. Your table data will be stored. See Figure 5-13.

Figure 5-13. *Inserting new records into a table*

Now it's time to add Entity Framework to your project.

Adding Entity Framework

Entity Framework is an ORM (object-relational mapping) framework; it gives users an automated mechanism for fetching and storing data into the database. Entity Framework is the extended version of ADO.NET.

In this demo, you already have one database and table so this situation will use a database-first approach. This is the approach developers choose when their database tables and stored procedures are already there and they want to consume them.

In the first step, you have to install Entity Framework core tools from the NuGet Package manager. So go to Tools ➤ NuGet Package Manager ➤ Package Manager Console. Run the following commands:

1. `PM>Install-Package Microsoft.EntityFrameworkCore.SqlServer`
2. `PM> Install-Package Microsoft.EntityFrameworkCore.Tools`

For the database-first approach, you must run the `Scaffold-DbContext` command in the Package Manager console window. Go to Tools ➤ NuGet Package Manager ➤ Package Manager Console. Run the following command:

```
Scaffold-DbContext "Server=(localdb)\MSSQLLocalDB;Database=SchoolDb;
Trusted_Connection=True;" Microsoft.EntityFrameworkCore.SqlServer
-OutputDir Models
```

Note that you must change the database name, server name, and trusted connection based on your requirements.

The following is a description of the above command:

- Scaffold-DbContext: This command produces an Entity Framework model for an existing database.

- Server: Database server name

- Database: The name of the database at the time of creation, such as SchoolDb

- Trusted_Connection: This is for using a Windows security trusted connection. If you want to set your database id and password, you have to remove this.

- –OutputDir: Name of the folder where you want to add your model classes and DbContext files

Once you run this command, it will generate two files for you in the Models folder:

- StudentMarks.cs

- StudentDbContext.cs

StudentMarks.cs is the model class for a table. In this demo, you created only one table, so you will get only one model class. If you create more tables based on your requirements, you will get more table files.

StudentDbContext.cs is related to table relationship mappings and a complete model of the database.

Now it's time to do some coding in the web API to fetch data from the table. Open StudentController.cs and copy the code in Listing 5-3 into it.

Listing 5-3. StudentController.cs

```
using System;
using System.Linq;
using Microsoft.AspNetCore.Mvc;
using WebApp.Models;
namespace WebApp.Controllers
```

```
{
 [Route("api/[controller]")]
 [ApiController]
public class StudentController : ControllerBase
 {
SchoolDbContext schoolDbContext = new SchoolDbContext();
[HttpGet]
public ActionResult GetStudents()
{
var query = schoolDbContext.StudentMarks.ToList();
return Ok(query);
 }
}
}
```

If you look at the code for StudentController.cs, one object is created for SchoolDbContext, which is responsible for connecting with the db and all tables, views, and stored procedures.

```
SchoolDbContext schoolDbContext = new SchoolDbContext();
```

Next, there's a method called GetStudents(). At the time of calling, this method will fetch the data from the db.

```
[HttpGet]
public ActionResult GetStudents()
 {
     var query = schoolDbContext.StudentMarks.ToList();
     return Ok(query);
 }
```

So here you create one variable named query and fetch the StudentMarks list into this variable. After that, there is a return OK(query), which means this will return an OK Negotiated Content result.

Now, it's time to run the web API. If you want to make this student controller method as your default API, it means whenever you run this project, it runs automatically, as do the below changes.

Go to Solution Explorer ➤ Properties ➤ Open launchSettings.json file and add the changes in Listing 5-4 to the `launchUrl` section.

Listing 5-4. launchSettings.json

```
{
"$schema": "http://json.schemastore.org/launchsettings.json",
"iisSettings": {
"windowsAuthentication": false,
"anonymousAuthentication": true,
"iisExpress": {
"applicationUrl": "http://localhost:54066",
"sslPort": 44396
    }
  },
"profiles": {
"IIS Express": {
"commandName": "IISExpress",
"launchBrowser": true,
"launchUrl": "api/student",
"environmentVariables": {
"ASPNETCORE_ENVIRONMENT": "Development"
      }
    },
"WebApp": {
"commandName": "Project",
"launchBrowser": true,
"launchUrl": "api/student",
"applicationUrl": "https://localhost:5001;http://localhost:5000",
"environmentVariables": {
"ASPNETCORE_ENVIRONMENT": "Development"
      }
    }
  }
}
```

In the code for `launchSettings.json`, note the change from `launchUrl` to `"api/student"`:

`"launchUrl": "api/student",`

The above step is totally up to you. If you want to skip this step, you can run your web API directly and change it in the browser address bar. To run your web API, go to Solution Explorer and right-click project ➤ Debug ➤ Start new instance. See Figure 5-14.

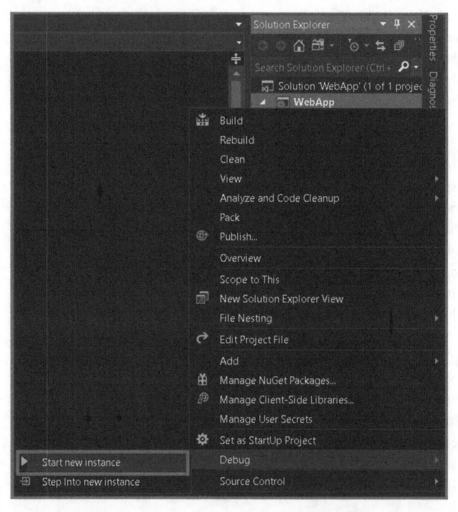

Figure 5-14. *Running the web API in a Visual Studio project*

Once you click the Start new instance button, it will run your project. Once you run the project, you will get the output in Figure 5-15.

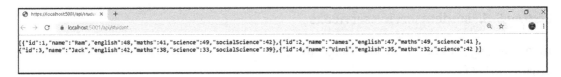

Figure 5-15. *api/student/getStudent returns data in the form of JSON*

As you can see in Figure 5-15, you got your response in the JSON format. Your API is running correctly, so you can fetch your data also. Now it's time to develop your Angular app to render the API data into Highcharts.

Angular-Highcharts UI Application

In Chapter 3, you created one Angular app. Here you'll continue with the same project, but you'll make some changes. Let's start to work on the Angular-Highcharts UI application.

Services in Angular

Services are code that can be accessed from multiple components. A service is defined for a purpose. If you want to make your code modularize and reusable, services are the best option. Services in Angular can be used as a repository. In the repository pattern, each service class is responsible for one purpose. For example, `StudentService` is responsible for student-related functions like `AddStudent()`, `UpdateStudent()`, and `GetStudentDetails()`.

Let's create a new service in Angular. Open the myFirstAngularHighchart application you created in Chapter 3. Now run the following command in a Visual Studio code terminal window to create a service:

`ng generate service service/studentservice`

This command will generate a new service with the name of `studentService` in the `service` folder (here the `service` folder is automatically created by this command).

Open `studentservice.service.ts` from the `service` folder and you will get the code in Listing 5-5.

Listing 5-5. studentservice.service.ts

```
import { Injectable } from '@angular/core';
@Injectable({
providedIn: 'root'
})
export class StudentserviceService{
constructor() { }
}
```

Let's review the code. In the first line, you can see an `Injectable` decorator. For this, you are using import for `Injectable` as in `import { Injectable } from '@angular/core'`.

You can see in the `Injectable` decorator you made as a root injector (`providedIn: 'root'`), which means this particular service is accessible from any component or any service level for this application.

Now you will create one model class to bind the data from the web API response. To create a model class, run the following command in Visual Studio:

ng generate class   model/marksModel

This command will generate one model class for you. Now paste the code in Listing 5-6 into the file.

Listing 5-6. marks-model.ts

```
export class MarksModel
{
english: string = "";
    maths: string = "";
    science: string = "";
    name: string = "";
}
```

In this code, there's one class called `MarksModel` and four properties. You can add more properties based on your requirements.

Now go back to the Studentservice.service.ts class. You will send a request to the web API project and get a response in the MarksModel class. Copy the complete code in Listing 5-7 into studentservice.service.ts.

Listing 5-7. studentservice.service.ts

```
import { Injectable } from '@angular/core';
import { HttpClient } from '@angular/common/http';
import { MarksModel } from '../model/marks-model';
import { Observable } from 'rxjs';
 @Injectable({
providedIn: 'root'
})
export class StudentserviceService {
constructor(private http: HttpClient) {
console.log('StudentserviceService called');
  }
Get(url: string): Observable<MarksModel[]> {
    return this.http.get<MarksModel[]>(url);
  }
}
```

Now let's understand the code. Here you add HttpClient. The HttpClient module is required for sending the request to the web API, so you add the following line:

import {HttpClient} from '@angular/common/http'

In the next line, you call MarksModel; as you know, you just created one Model class. In the next line, you call Observable from RxJs.

Observable helps your application pass messages between publishers and subscribers. Here a method never executes until consumers subscribe to it. Observable can handle any type of value like messages, literals, and events.

Observable is used to retrieve data. Observable helps handle asynchronous data, such as data coming from a back-end database or service. Here events are treated as a collection.

RxJs stands for Reactive Extensions for JavaScript, and it is used for asynchronous programming using Observable. With RxJs you can work on the server side with Node.js or on the browser side. Here *asynchronous* means you will call your method and register for notifications when results are available, so with this approach, your web page will never become unresponsive.

Now look at the constructor level. You inject HttpClient (this is the best example of dependency injection in Angular) so you can send a get request to the web API.

```
constructor(private http: HttpClient) {
 }
```

Then you have a Get method where you send the http.get request. There is a Get(url) method with one parameter, url. This url comes from the caller, which is a component in this application.

Once this method gets its url, it will send a http.get request to the web API. The method return type is MarksModel[] array because from a web API you get data in the form of a collection, which is why you're using an array here. In this case, the URL will be https://localhost:5001/api/student.

(Note: Your port number may change, so please provide the proper port number. Refer to Figure 5-15.)

In Figure 5-15, you can see the URL of https://localhost:5001/api/student. If you want to access the student API, you have to call this particular URL.

```
Get(url: string): Observable<MarksModel[]> {
    return this.http.get<MarksModel[]>(url);
 }
```

Now it's time to call httpClient in the app.module.ts level, so add HttpClientModule because it's required to access the web API. Copy the code in Listing 5-8 into the app.module.ts file.

Listing 5-8. app.module.ts

```
import { BrowserModule } from '@angular/platform-browser';
import { NgModule } from '@angular/core';
import {HttpClientModule} from '@angular/common/http';
import { AppRoutingModule } from './app-routing.module';
import { AppComponent } from './app.component';
```

114

```
import { HighchartsChartComponent } from 'highcharts-angular';
  @NgModule({
  declarations: [
  AppComponent,
  HighchartsChartComponent,
  ],
  imports: [
  BrowserModule,
  HttpClientModule,
  AppRoutingModule
  ],
 //providers: [StudentserviceService],
  bootstrap: [AppComponent]
  })
  export class AppModule{ }
```

Now it's time to work on the component level. Copy the code in Listing 5-9 into the student-marks.component.ts file.

Listing 5-9. student-marks.component.ts

```
import { Component, OnInit } from '@angular/core';
import { MarksModel } from '../model/marks-model';
import { StudentserviceService } from '../services/studentservice.service';
import * as Highcharts from 'highcharts';

@Component({
  selector: 'app-student-marks',
templateUrl: './student-marks.component.html',
styleUrls: ['./student-marks.component.css']
})
export class StudentMarksComponent {
studentModel: MarksModel[] = [];
  url: string = 'https://localhost:7050/api/Student';
studentNames: any;
constructor(private studentservice: StudentserviceService) {
  }
```

115

```typescript
  public options: any = {
    chart: {
      type: 'line',
    },
    title: {
      text: 'Real Time Data Example'
    },
    credits: {
      enabled: false
    },
xAxis: {
      categories: ['English', 'Maths', 'Science']
    },
yAxis: {
      title: {
        text: 'Marks'
      },
    },
    series: [],
  }
ngOnInit() {
this.getApiResponse(this.url).then(
      data => {
constsubjectMarks:any = [];
const names: any = [];
data?.forEach(row => {
consttemp_row = [
row.english,
row.maths,
row.science
        ];
names.push(row.name);
subjectMarks.push(temp_row);
      });
this.studentModel = subjectMarks;
```

```
this.studentNames = names;
        var dataSeries = [];
        for (var i = 0; i<this.studentModel.length; i++) {
dataSeries.push({
            data: this.studentModel[i],
            name: this.studentNames[i]
          });
        }
this.options.series = dataSeries;
Highcharts.chart('container', this.options);
      },
        error => {
console.log('Something went wrong.');
      })
  }
getApiResponse(url:string) {
    return this.studentservice.Get(this.url)
.toPromise().then(res => {
        return res;
      });
  }
}
```

Let's understand Listing 5-9 line by line. This code is an enhancement of
the component you developed in Chapters 3 and 4. You import MarksModel and
studentserviceService for reference.

```
import { MarksModel } from '../model/marks-model';
import { StudentserviceService } from '../services/studentservice.service';
```

Next are three variables: studentModel, url, and studentNames. studentModel is
for fetching marks data from service, url is for sending the request to the web API, and
studentNames is for collecting names.

```
studentModel: MarksModel[] = [];
  url: string = 'https://localhost:7050/api/Student';
studentNames: any;
```

Then you inject (an example of dependency injection) `studentserviceService` into a constructor.

```
constructor(private studentservice: StudentserviceService) {
  }
```

Then you write code for Highcharts, where you define all basic properties for the chart in the options.

In the last section of code, you create one method with the name of `getApiResponse(url)`; this method is responsible for sending the request to `studentService Get()` method. See the following code:

```
getApiResponse(url:string) {
    return this.studentservice.Get(this.url)
.toPromise().then(res => {
        return res;
      });
```

Now let's talk about the `ngOnInit()` function. This function starts to run in the Angular lifecycle when the component load completes, so you can say it's a page load kind of event method. Once `student-marks.component.ts` loads, this method will start to execute.

```
ngOnInit() {
this.getApiResponse(this.url).then(
        data => {
constsubjectMarks:any = [];
const names: any = [];
data?.forEach(row => {
consttemp_row = [
row.english,
row.maths,
row.science
        ];
names.push(row.name);
subjectMarks.push(temp_row);
      });
this.studentModel = subjectMarks;
```

```
this.studentNames = names;
        var dataSeries = [];
        for (var i = 0; i<this.studentModel.length; i++) {
dataSeries.push({
            data: this.studentModel[i],
            name: this.studentNames[i]
          });
        }
this.options.series = dataSeries;
Highcharts.chart('container', this.options);
      },
      error => {
console.log('Something went wrong.');
      })
  }
```

In the ngOnInit() code, you call the getApiResponse(url) method. This method calls studentService and gets a response with the use of the array.ForEach loop, storing records one by one into the temp_row variable.

In the next step, you push this list into the studentNames and studentMarks array type variables. In the dataSeries, which is the most important part for constructing a chart, you define the data and name properties, so the data property will construct in this way. See the following code:

```
[{
name: 'StudentName1',
data: [marks1, marks2, marks3]
    }, {
name: 'StudentName2',
data: [marks1, marks2, marks3]
    }, {
name: 'StudentName3',
data: [marks1, marks2, marks3]
    }, {
name: 'StudentName4',
data: [marks1, marks2, marks3]
}],
```

And then you define `options.series`, and in the next line, call `Highcharts.chart` to construct a `'container <div>'`.

Now it's time to write code into `student-marks.component.html`. Copy the code in Listing 5-10 into the `app.component.html` file.

Listing 5-10. student-marks.component.html

```
<div class="content" id="container" role="main">
  </div>
  <router-outlet></router-outlet>
```

Now type `ng serve` and press Enter. Type `localhost:4200` in your browser and press Enter. At this point, you will get no output. Press F12 to troubleshoot this problem. Once you press F12 in your browser, you will get the screen in Figure 5-16.

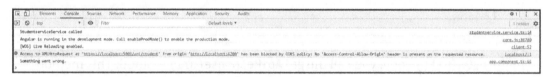

Figure 5-16. *Press F12 to troubleshoot CORS issues*

Figure 5-16 shows this as an issue of CORS, which stands for *cross-origin resource sharing*. Whenever you send the request in two different resources or projects, you get this problem.

Here two different projects mean one project for Web API and one project for an Angular app. CORS is an approach that allows restricted resources on a web page.

If you see the browser error, it clearly says Access to XMLHttpRequest at http://localhost:5001/api/student (this URL is from the web API project) from origin http://localhost:4200 (this is from the Angular app) has been blocked by CORS policy because no access-control-allow-origin header is present on the requested resource.

For the requested resource, which is the web API, you have to add a CORS policy. For this, you permit localhost:4200 because this is your Angular app URL. So, stop your web API project and follow these steps.

Step 1. Add `Microsoft.AspNetCore.Cors` from the NuGet package.

Step 2. If you are working with .NET 6 or more, please add the following code into `program.cs` (for this example, I am using .NET 6.):

```
string CORSOpenPolicy = "AddCORSPolicy";

builder.Services.AddCors();

builder.Services.AddCors(options =>
{
options.AddPolicy(
        name: CORSOpenPolicy,
        builder => {
builder.WithOrigins("*").AllowAnyHeader().AllowAnyMethod();
        });
});
app.UseCors(CORSOpenPolicy);
```

In this code, first you declare a variable called `CorsOpenPolicy`. You use this string variable in the web API controller and in the place of adding a Cors name. In the next step, you add a Cors policy into services. Then there are properties like `withOrigin`, `AllowAnyHeader`, and `AllowAnyMethod`. These fields are required for setting `url`, `header`, and `method` types like `get`, `put`, `post`, and `delete`. So based on your requirements, you can set them. Lastly is `useCors`, which denotes whatever policy the API has to follow.

For your complete reference, Listing 5-11 contains the full code of `program.cs`. If you face any issue, paste in the entire code into `program.cs`.

Listing 5-11. program.cs

```
var builder = WebApplication.CreateBuilder(args);
string CORSOpenPolicy = "AddCORSPolicy";
// Add services to the container.
builder.Services.AddControllers();
// Learn more about configuring Swagger/OpenAPI at https://aka.ms/
aspnetcore/swashbuckle
builder.Services.AddEndpointsApiExplorer();
builder.Services.AddSwaggerGen();
builder.Services.AddCors();
```

```
builder.Services.AddCors(options =>
{
options.AddPolicy(
        name: CORSOpenPolicy,
        builder => {
builder.WithOrigins("*").AllowAnyHeader().AllowAnyMethod();
        });
});
var app = builder.Build();
// Configure the HTTP request pipeline.
if (app.Environment.IsDevelopment())
{
app.UseSwagger();
app.UseSwaggerUI();
}
app.UseCors(CORSOpenPolicy);
app.UseHttpsRedirection();
app.UseAuthorization();
app.MapControllers();
app.Run();
```

Open the StudentController.cs file and add the following code above
[Route("api/[controller]")] attribute route.

```
[EnableCors("AddCORSPolicy")]
```

Now run your Web API project again and run the Angular app. You will get the
output shown in Figure 5-17.

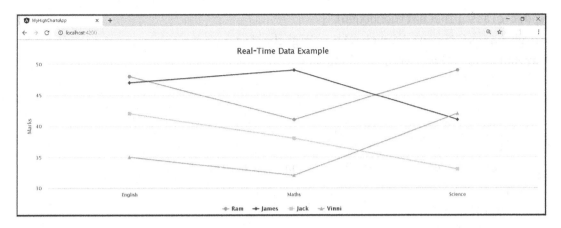

Figure 5-17. *Real-time line chart with a back-end web API*

The current data is coming from a back-end service. To call a back-end service, it's not necessary to call the web API. You can send the request to a PHP service or any web service you prefer; all you need is a URL. If your URL is correct and if you know the response type, you can fetch data very easily.

Events in Highcharts

Events are the essential part of an application. With the use of these events, the app can react to actions like click events, mouse-over events, load events, and `legendItemClicks`. In this section, I will talk about events. An event can be generated in Highcharts through an event property. Let's see an example. This example is a simple line chart. When you click on the points, you will get alert box with data.

Copy the code in Listing 5-12 into the `line-chart.component.ts` file.

Listing 5-12. line-chart.component.ts

```
import { Component, OnInit } from '@angular/core';
import * as Highcharts from 'highcharts';

@Component({
  selector: 'app-line-chart',
templateUrl: './line-chart.component.html',
styleUrls: ['./line-chart.component.css']
})
```

123

```
export class LineChartComponent {
  Highcharts: typeof Highcharts = Highcharts;
chartOptions: Highcharts.Options = {
    chart: {
      type: "line"
    },
    title: {
      text: "Monthly Sales Chart Department Wise"
    },
    subtitle: {
      text: "Year 2022"
    },
xAxis: {
      categories: ["Jan", "Feb", "Mar", "Apr", "May", "Jun",
        "Jul", "Aug", "Sep", "Oct", "Nov", "Dec"]
    },
yAxis: {
      title: {
        text: "Sales in Million $"
      }
    },
    series: [{
      type: "line",
      name: 'Marketing Department',
      data: [49.9, 51.5, 32.0, 82.0, 75.0, 66.0, 32.0, 25.0,
        35.4, 65.1, 58.6, 34.4],
      point: {
        events: {
          click: function () {
alert('Name: ' + this.series.name + ' = ' + this.y);
          }
        }
      }
    },
```

```
        ],
    };
}
```

Run Listing 5-12's code with ng serve, and you will get the output in Figure 5-18. Click any series and you will get an alert with the name, subject, and marks of a student.

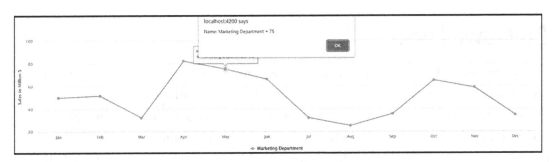

Figure 5-18. *Chart series with a plotOptions series click event*

Let's understand Listing 5-12's code. As you know, this is the continuation of the last demo, but here you add a few new things to generate click events. First, you add the following code into options area for creating Highcharts:

```
series: [{
        type: "line",
        name: 'Marketing Department',
        data: [49.9, 51.5, 32.0, 82.0, 75.0, 66.0, 32.0, 25.0,
         35.4, 65.1, 58.6, 34.4],
        point: {
         events: {
            click: function () {
alert('Name: ' + this.series.name + ' = ' + this.y);
            }
          }
        }
    },
    ],
```

In the series, you add a point, and then you add events, such as a click event. For this click event, you have the method, so once a user clicks a series point, this function will activate.

After clicking the series, it will display the name of a department and sales value in an alert box (Figure 5-18).

Drilldown Event

A drilldown event fires when you click the chart, and you will get the detailing of that particular series. You can add this detailing into any chart with the use of the drilldown event. In the upcoming example, you will see three types of software: operating systems, programming languages, and browsers. When the user clicks one series, it will show the percentage of how much that product is used worldwide. See the code in Listing 5-13 (add this code to `drill-down-event.component.ts`).

Listing 5-13. drill-down-event.component.ts

```
import { Component, OnInit } from '@angular/core';
import * as Highcharts from 'highcharts';
import Drilldown from 'highcharts/modules/drilldown';
Drilldown(Highcharts);

@Component({
  selector: 'app-drill-down-event',
templateUrl: './drill-down-event.component.html',
styleUrls: ['./drill-down-event.component.css']
})

export class DrillDownEventComponent {
  Highcharts: typeof Highcharts = Highcharts;

drilldownData = {
    series: [{
      type: 'column',
      id: 'programminglanguage',
```

```
      data: [
        ['C#', 60],
        ['Java', 40]
      ]
    }, {
      type: 'column',
      id: 'operatingsystem',
      data: [
        ['Windows', 80],
        ['Linux', 20]
      ]
    }, {
      type: 'column',
      id: 'browser',
      data: [
        ['Chrome', 70],
        ['IE', 10],
        ['FireFox', 20],
      ]
    }]
  } as Highcharts.DrilldownOptions

chartOptions: Highcharts.Options = {
    chart: {
      events: {
        drilldown: () => {
          console.log(this.drilldownData);
        }
      }
    },
    title: {
      text: 'Software Products used Worldwide in Percentage',
    },
xAxis: {
    type: 'category'
        },
```

```
plotOptions: {
        series: {
borderWidth: 0,
dataLabels: {
        enabled: true
                }
             }
           },
     series: [{
        type: 'column',
        name: 'Softwares',
colorByPoint: true,
        data: [{
          name: 'ProgrammingLanguage',
          y: 2,
          drilldown: 'programminglanguage'
        }, {
          name: 'OperatingSystem',
          y: 2,
          drilldown: 'operatingsystem'
        }, {
          name: 'Browser',
          y: 3,
          drilldown: 'browser'
        }]
     }],
     drilldown: this.drilldownData
  };
}
```

Let's go through the code. As you know, to work on the drilldown feature, you must import the Drilldown dependency.

```
import Drilldown from 'highcharts/modules/drilldown';
Drilldown(Highcharts);
```

In the next step, you must call a series.

```
series: [{
      type: 'column',
      name: 'Softwares',
colorByPoint: true,
      data: [{
        name: 'ProgrammingLanguage',
        y: 2,
        drilldown: 'programminglanguage'
      }, {
        name: 'OperatingSystem',
        y: 2,
        drilldown: 'operatingsystem'
      }, {
        name: 'Browser',
        y: 3,
        drilldown: 'browser'
      }]
    }],
```

Here you use a name property. This name becomes the id for that particular series for the detailing part because in a drilldown you must show details of that specific chart. Now you add the events method.

```
drilldownData = {
    series: [{
        type: 'column',
        id: 'programminglanguage',
        data: [
          ['C#', 60],
          ['Java', 40]
        ]
    }, {
        type: 'column',
        id: 'operatingsystem',
```

```
    data: [
      ['Windows', 80],
      ['Linux', 20]
    ]
  }, {
    type: 'column',
    id: 'browser',
    data: [
      ['Chrome', 70],
      ['IE', 10],
      ['FireFox', 20],
    ]
  }]
} as Highcharts.DrilldownOptions
drilldown: this.drilldownData
```

Note that the name property is the same as the series because in the series variable you call `drilldown`. This array provides the details of that particular series.

```
drilldown: this.drilldownData
```

Now copy the code in Listing 5-14 into the `drill-down-event.component.html` file.

Listing 5-14. drill-down-event.component.html

```
<div class="content" role="main">
<highcharts-chart [Highcharts]="Highcharts"
    [options]="chartOptions"
        style="width: 100%; height: 400px; display: block;">
</highcharts-chart>
</div>
<router-outlet></router-outlet>
```

Type ng serve into a terminal window and your code will start running. See Figure 5-19.

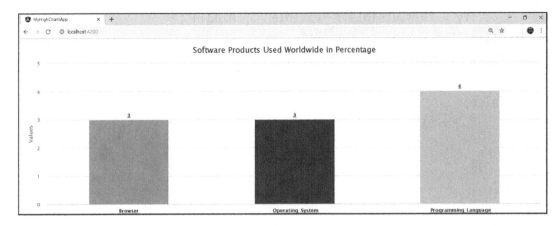

Figure 5-19. *Bar chart with drilldown event*

Click on the chart. You will get details of the particular series you clicked. In Figure 5-20, there is a menu link called Softwares/Browser. Once you click this button, it will redirect to the main chart.

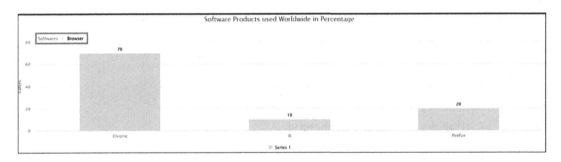

Figure 5-20. *Drilldown event detail screen*

legendItemClick Event

The legendItemClick event fires once you click a legend. This action is passed to the method. You set visibility to true or false in a toggle way. See the Listing 5-15 code.

Listing 5-15. app.component.ts

```
plotOptions: {
series: {
events: {
legendItemClick: function () {
```

131

```
var visibility = this.visible ? 'visible' : 'hidden';
if (!confirm('The series is currently ' +
visibility + '. Want to change it ?'))
          {
return false;
                }
              }
            }
          }
        },
```

As you can see in the Listing 5-15 code, in the `plotOptions.series` you add events as `legendItemClick()`.

Once the user clicks the legend, it will check whether the legend for this particular series is visible or not. The message will generate based on the visibility of a series.

If the user clicks the OK button, the action will occur. If the user clicks the Cancel button, nothing will happen. Now copy the full code in Listing 5-16 into the legend-click.component.ts file.

Listing 5-16. legend-click.component.ts

```
import { Component, OnInit } from '@angular/core';
import * as Highcharts from 'highcharts';

interface ExtendXAxis extends Highcharts.XAxisOptions {
  categories: any;
}
 @Component({
  selector: 'app-legend-click',
templateUrl: './legend-click.component.html',
styleUrls: ['./legend-click.component.css']
})
export class LegendClickComponent {
  Highcharts: typeof Highcharts = Highcharts;
chartOptions: Highcharts.Options = {
    chart: {
      type: "line"
    },
```

```
    title: {
      text: 'Industry Growth by Sector, 2014-2019'
    },
xAxis: {
      categories: [2014, 2015, 2016, 2017, 2018, 2019],
      } as ExtendXAxis,
yAxis: {
      title: {
        text: 'Revenue Generated in million'
      }
    },
    legend: {
      layout: 'vertical',
      align: 'right',
verticalAlign: 'middle'
    },
plotOptions: {
      series: {
        events: {
legendItemClick: function () {
            var visibility = this.visible ? 'visible' :
              'hidden';
            if (!confirm('The series is currently ' +
              visibility + '. Want to change that ?')) {
              return false;
            }
            else
            {
              return true;
            }
          }
        }
      }
    },
```

```
      series: [{
        type: "line",
        name: 'IT',
        data: [400, 489, 354, 180, 785, 293]
      }, {
        type: "line",
        name: 'Cement',
        data: [180, 100, 50, 89, 105, 206]
      }, {
        type: "line",
        name: 'Pharmacy',
        data: [350, 400, 250, 400, 550, 480]
      }, {
        type: "line",
        name: 'Agriculture',
        data: [190, 210, 250, 280, 310, 500]
      }],
    }
}
```

Run the Listing 5-16 code with ng serve and you will get the output shown in
Figure 5-21.

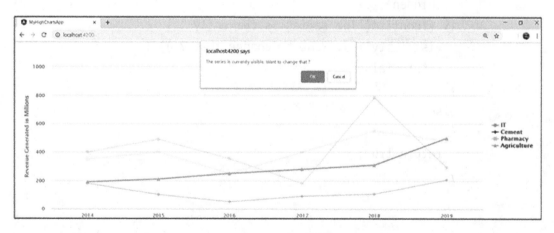

Figure 5-21. *legendItemClick event using HighCharts*

CheckBoxClick Event

The CheckBoxClick() event fires once a user clicks the checkbox visible next to the legend section of a chart. A Checkboxclick event will fire once the user has checked or unchecked it. You can write your logic based on your requirements. See Listing 5-17.

In this example, once the user clicks the legend checkbox, based on whether it is checked or unchecked, it will display a message in the chart area about the particular series.

Listing 5-17. checkbox-click-event.component.ts

```
plotOptions: {
      series: {
         events: {
checkboxClick: function (event) {
const chart: ExtendedChart = this.chart;
            var text;
            if (event.checked == true) {
               text = 'The checkbox is now checked and Series Label is ' +
               this.name;
            }
            else {
text = 'The checkbox is now unchecked and Series Label is ' + this.name;
            }
            if (!chart.lbl) {
chart.lbl = this.chart.renderer.label(text, 100, 70)
.attr({
                  padding: 10,
                  r: 5,
                  fill: 'lightblue',
zIndex: 5
               })
               .css({
color: 'white'
               })
.add();
```

```
        } else {
chart.lbl.attr({
              text: text
          });
        }
      }
    },
showCheckbox: true
    }
  },
```

In Listing 5-17, there is a property called showcheckbox: true. This is the first step to show a checkbox next to a legend.

In the next part, in the event section, you call the checkboxclick() method event. In event.checked, you get a value of true or false. If the checkbox is checked, you will get true; otherwise, you get false. Based on that, you write the logic.

For the full code, copy Listing 5-18's code into the checkbox-click-event. component.ts file.

Listing 5-18. checkbox-click-event.component.ts

```typescript
import { Component, OnInit } from '@angular/core';
import * as Highcharts from 'highcharts';

interface ExtendedChart extends Highcharts.Chart {
lbl?:Highcharts.SVGElement;
}

interface ExtendXAxisOption extends Highcharts.XAxisOptions
{
categories : any;
}

@Component({
  selector: 'app-checkbox-click-event',
templateUrl: './checkbox-click-event.component.html',
styleUrls: ['./checkbox-click-event.component.css']
})
```

```typescript
export class CheckboxClickEventComponent {
  Highcharts: typeof Highcharts = Highcharts;
chartOptions: Highcharts.Options = {
    chart: {
      type: "line"
    },
    title: {
      text: 'Industry Growth by Sector, 2018-2023'
    },
xAxis: {
      categories: [2018, 2019, 2020, 2021, 2022, 2023],
    }as ExtendXAxisOption,
yAxis: {
      title: {
        text: 'Revenue Generated in million'
      }
    },
    legend: {
      layout: 'vertical',
      align: 'right',
verticalAlign: 'middle'
    },
plotOptions: {
      series: {
        events: {
checkboxClick: function (event) {
const chart: ExtendedChart = this.chart;
            var text;
            if (event.checked == true) {
              text = 'The checkbox is now checked and Series Label is ' +
              this.name;
            }
            else {
              text = 'The checkbox is now unchecked and Series Label is '
              + this.name;
            }
```

```
                if (!chart.lbl) {
chart.lbl = this.chart.renderer.label(text, 100, 70)
.attr({
                    padding: 10,
                    r: 5,
                    fill: 'lightblue',
zIndex: 5
                })
                .css({
color: 'white'
                })
.add();
                } else {
chart.lbl.attr({
                    text: text
                });
                }
            }
        },
showCheckbox: true
        }
    },
    series: [{
      type: 'line',
      name: 'IT',
      data: [400, 489, 354, 180, 785, 293]
    }, {
      type: 'line',
      name: 'Cement',
      data: [180, 100, 50, 89, 105, 206]
    }, {
      type: 'line',
      name: 'Pharmacy',
      data: [350, 400, 250, 400, 550, 480]
    }, {
```

```
    type: 'line',
    name: 'Agriculture',
    data: [190, 210, 250, 280, 310, 500]
  }],
  }
}
```

Once you run the code with ng serve, you will get the output seen in Figure 5-22.

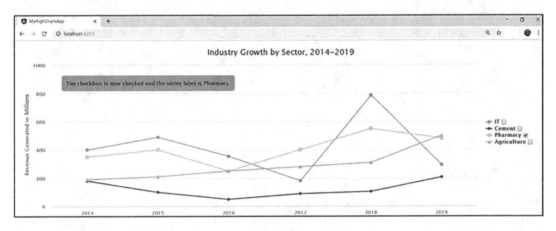

Figure 5-22. *CheckBoxClick event using HighCharts*

Highcharts Wrapper for .NET

The Highcharts wrapper is an API that is available for almost all significant frameworks like Highcharts IOS, Highcharts Android, Highcharts Angular, Highcharts React, Highcharts React Native, and HighchartsVue (for Vue.js).

In this section, I will talk about the Highcharts wrapper for .NET; this is an API that provides full support for the .NET Framework. Now developers can write code without JavaScript. If you are an ASP.NET MVC developer and you want to develop your charting without JavaScript, you can build through the Highcharts API.

In this section, I will show you two examples: a line series chart and gauge chart with a Highcharts wrapper.

Line Series Chart with a Highcharts Wrapper

Follow these steps:

- **Step 1**: Create an ASP.NET MVC application through Visual Studio.

- **Step 2**: Go to Solution Explorer. Right-click the MVC project and select Manage NuGet packages from the menu. See Figure 5-23.

Figure 5-23. *Installing the Highcharts API using NuGet in Visual Studio*

- **Step 3**: Click Browse, search Highsoft.Web.Mvc.Charts ➤ Select Highsoft.Web.Mvc, and click the Install button (Figure 5-23).

- **Step 4**: Go to Solution Explorer. Open Dependencies ➤ NuGet section. You can see `Highsoft.Web.Mvc`.

- **Step 5**: Go to the controller and paste the code in Listing 5-19 into the Index method. For this demo, use `HomeController.cs`.

Listing 5-19. HomeController.cs

```
using Microsoft.AspNetCore.Mvc;
using Highsoft.Web.Mvc.Charts;
using System.Diagnostics;
using System.Collections.Generic;
```

```
using WebApplication1.Models;

namespace WebApplication1.Controllers
{
 public class HomeController : Controller
    {
        private readonlyILogger<HomeController> _logger;
        public HomeController()
        {

        }
        public HomeController(ILogger<HomeController> logger)
        {
            _logger = logger;
        }

        public ActionResult Index()
        {
          List<double> marketingDepartmentCollection = new List<double>{
          49.9, 51.5, 32.0, 82.0, 75.0, 66.0, 32.0, 25.0, 35.4, 65.1,
          58.6, 34.4 };
          List<double> CsDepartmentCollection = new List<double>{
          40.5, 34.5, 84.4, 39.2, 23.2, 45.0, 55.6, 18.5, 26.4, 14.1,
          23.6, 84.4 };
          List<LineSeriesData> marketingData = new List<LineSeriesData>();
          List<LineSeriesData> CsData = new List<LineSeriesData>();
marketingDepartmentCollection.ForEach(p =>marketingData.Add(new
LineSeriesData{ Y = p }));
CsDepartmentCollection.ForEach(p =>CsData.Add(new LineSeriesData{ Y = p }));
ViewData["marketingData"] = marketingData;
ViewData["CsData"] = CsData;
            return View();
        }

    }
}
```

In this code, you see lists for the Marketing and Computer Science departments, and you develop a line chart.

For this demo, use a `LineSeriesData` class. If you want to create an area chart or pie chart, you must call the related classes like `AreaSeriesData` or `PieSeriesData`.

A later section will talk about series data classes for the Highcharts API. For this `LineSeriesData`, it gets the collection in the form of series data; you send this to the `ViewBag` collection memory. `ViewBag` is required when you want to transmit your values from the controller to a view. Now it will work on the UI side, so open View folder ➤ Home folder ➤ index.cshtml and paste in the code seen in Listing 5-20.

Listing 5-20. index.cshtml

```
@{
ViewBag.Title = "Home Page";
}
<script src="https://code.highcharts.com/highcharts.js"></script>
@using Highsoft.Web.Mvc.Charts
@using Highsoft.Web.Mvc.Charts.Rendering;
@{var chartOptions = new Highcharts
    {
        Title = new Title
        {
            Text = "Monthly Sales Chart Department Wise",
        },
        Legend = new Legend
        {
            Layout = LegendLayout.Vertical,
            Align = LegendAlign.Right,
VerticalAlign = LegendVerticalAlign.Middle,
BorderWidth = 0
        },
        Subtitle = new Subtitle
        {
            Text = "Year 2023",
        },
```

```
XAxis = new List<XAxis>
{
new XAxis
  {
    Categories = new List<string>{ "Jan", "Feb", "Mar", "Apr", "May",
    "Jun","Jul", "Aug", "Sep", "Oct", "Nov", "Dec" },
    }
  },
YAxis = new List<YAxis>
{
new YAxis
      {
PlotLines = new List<YAxisPlotLines>
{
new YAxisPlotLines
                      {
                          Value = 0,
                          Width = 1,
Color = "red"
                      }
                  }
              }
          },
      Series = new List<Series>
{
new LineSeries
              {
                  Name = "Marketing Department",
 Data = @ViewData["marketingData"] as List<LineSeriesData>
              },
new LineSeries
              {
                  Name = "Computer Science Department",
Data = @ViewData["CsData"] as List<LineSeriesData>
              },
```

```
            }
        };
        chartOptions.ID = "chart";
        var renderer = new HighchartsRenderer(chartOptions);
}
@Html.Raw(renderer.RenderHtml())
```

As you can see in the above code, no JavaScript code is required. You work only with Razor and C#-based classes. Here you have one variable called `chartOptions`, and this variable is called to render Highcharts:

```
var renderer = new HighchartsRenderer(chartOptions);
```

Once you run the above code using Visual Studio, you will get the output seen in Figure 5-24.

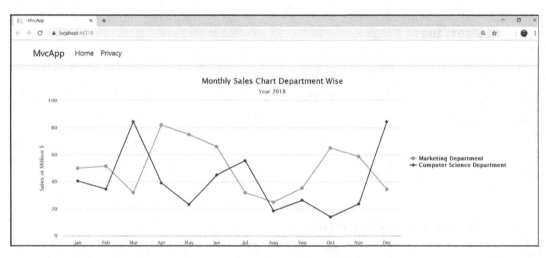

Figure 5-24. *Highcharts API demo with the .NET Framework*

Gauge Chart with a Highcharts Wrapper

For developing a gauge, the `GaugeSeriesData` class is required. For more understanding, copy Listing 5-21 code into the `HomeController.cs` file.

Listing 5-21. HomeController.cs

```
using Microsoft.AspNetCore.Mvc;
using Highsoft.Web.Mvc.Charts;
using System.Collections.Generic;
namespace MvcApp.Controllers
{
public class HomeController : Controller
    {
        private readonly ILogger<HomeController> _logger;
        public HomeController()
        {
        }
        public HomeController(ILogger<HomeController> logger)
        {
            _logger = logger;
        }
        public ActionResult Index()
        {
List<GaugeSeriesData> gaugeData = new List<GaugeSeriesData>();
gaugeData.Add(new GaugeSeriesData{ Y = 60 });
ViewData["gaugeData"] = gaugeData;
            return View();
        }
    }
}
```

In Listing 5-21, you use the GaugeSeriesData class. As you know, in a gauge chart you must set a starting value, so here the value is 60. Whenever you run this code, the starting value will be 60. The next part is the UI. Copy the code in Listing 5-22 into index.cshtml.

Listing 5-22. index.cshtml

```
@{
ViewBag.Title = "Home Page";
}
```

```
 <script src="https://code.highcharts.com/highcharts.js"></script>
<script src="https://code.highcharts.com/highcharts-more.js"></script>
@using Highsoft.Web.Mvc.Charts
@using Highsoft.Web.Mvc.Charts.Rendering
@{var chartOptions = new Highcharts
      {
          Chart = new Highsoft.Web.Mvc.Charts.Chart
          {
PlotBorderColor = null,
PlotBackgroundImage = null,
PlotBorderWidth = 0,
PlotShadow = new Shadow
              {
                    Enabled = false
              }
          },
          Title = new Title
          {
              Text = "Speedometer"
          },
          Pane = new Pane
          {
StartAngle = -150,
EndAngle = 150
          },
YAxis = new List<YAxis>
{
new YAxis
                  {
                    Min = 0,
                    Max = 200,
MinorTickWidth = 1,
MinorTickLength = 10,
MinorTickPosition = YAxisMinorTickPosition.Inside,
MinorTickColor = "#666",
```

```
TickPixelInterval = 30,
TickWidth = 2,
TickPosition = YAxisTickPosition.Inside,
TickLength = 10,
TickColor = "#666",
                    Labels = new YAxisLabels
                    {
                        Step = 2
                    },
                    Title = new YAxisTitle
                    {
                        Text = "km/h"
                    },
PlotBands = new List<YAxisPlotBands>
{
new YAxisPlotBands
                        {
                            From = 0,
                            To = 120,
Color = "#55BF3B"
                        },
new YAxisPlotBands
                        {
                            From = 120,
                            To = 150,
                        },
new YAxisPlotBands
                        {
                            From = 150,
                            To = 200,
Color = "#DF5353"
                        }
                    }
                }
            },
```

```
        Series = new List<Series>
{
new GaugeSeries
        {
            Name = "Speed",
            Data = @ViewData["gaugeData"] as List<GaugeSeriesData>,
            Tooltip = new GaugeSeriesTooltip
            {
ValueSuffix = " km/h"
            }
        }
    }
    };
    chartOptions.ID = "chart";
    var renderer = new HighchartsRenderer(chartOptions);
}
@Html.Raw(renderer.RenderHtml())
<script type="text/javascript">
window.setTimeout(function () {
        var chart = Highcharts.charts[0];
        if (!chart.renderer.forExport) {
setInterval(function () {
                var point = chart.series[0].points[0],
newVal,
inc = Math.round((Math.random() - 0.7) * 30);
newVal = point.y + inc;
                if (newVal< 0 || newVal> 200) {
newVal = point.y - inc;
                }
point.update(newVal);
        }, 1000);
    }
    }, 1000);
</script>
```

In Listing 5-22, you create a gauge chart using the Highcharts class. After that, you use JavaScript code to generate a gauge event using the `window.setTimeout`, so the value of the gauge chart is changed every second.

```javascript
window.setTimeout(function () {
var chart = Highcharts.charts[0];
if (!chart.renderer.forExport) {
setInterval(function () {
var point = chart.series[0].points[0],
newVal,
inc = Math.round((Math.random() - 0.7) * 30);
newVal = point.y + inc;
if (newVal< 0 || newVal> 200) {
newVal = point.y - inc;
                }
point.update(newVal);
          }, 1000);
      }
   }, 1000);
```

Run the above code and you will get the output seen in Figure 5-25. The meter changes every second.

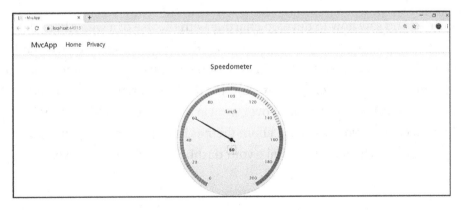

Figure 5-25. *Gauge chart with a Highcharts wrapper API for .NET*

149

SeriesData Classes

The Highcharts API wrapper is available for different frameworks, and you have to install those dependencies based on your requirements. Refer to Table 5-1.

Table 5-1. *Chart Type SeriesData Classes for Working with a Highcharts API in the .NET Framework*

Class Name	Use
LineSeriesData	For drawing line-type charts and generating a series for line components. You already saw an example of this.
AreaSeriesData	For generating an area-type chart with series data for an area chart
SplineSeriesData	For generating a spline-type chart with series data for a spline chart
BarSeriesData	For generating a bar-type chart with series data for a bar chart
ColumnSeriesData	For generating a column-type chart with series data for a column chart
PieSeriesData	For generating a pie-type chart with series data for the pie chart
ScatterSeriesData	For generating a scatter-type chart with series data for a scatter chart

Summary

In this chapter, you saw how to develop charting with the use of a web API and the Angular service with the REST pattern. You can send the request to any back-end service with an HTTP client; you just need a URL and its return type. You can add events on your charting script very easily; events are executed in the browser once any related action happens, such as a click event, mouse over, mouse up, or checked legend click.

In the next chapter, you will learn about themes in Highcharts and additional features provided by Highcharts to make your dashboard more interactive.

CHAPTER 6

Themes and Additional Features of Highcharts

Sourabh Mishra[a*]

[a] IECE Digital, Bangalore, India

In this chapter, you are going to learn about themes, styles, and additional features of Highcharts. You will also learn how to export your charts in different formats. Additionally, you'll learn about 3D charting and Highcharts Gantt. Highcharts Gantt is newly introduced by the Highcharts team. These features will make your dashboard rich and more interactive, so let's begin this chapter.

Themes in Highcharts

In computer science, themes are a set of packages of colors and graphical representations. In Highcharts, you can define your theme. Here's how to set styles and themes for Highcharts:

- `Axis`: You can add styles to the x-axis and the y-axis.

- `alternateGridColor`: You can set this property for the x-axis and the y-axis. This will add a color band alternatively across the chart plot base on the axis. See Listing 6-1.

© Sourabh Mishra 2023
S. Mishra, *Practical Highcharts with Angular*, https://doi.org/10.1007/978-1-4842-9181-8_6

Listing 6-1. app.component.ts

```
yAxis: {
        alternateGridColor: 'red'
    },
    xAxis: {
        alternateGridColor: 'green'
    },
```

- gridLineColor: This sets a primary grid line color for an axis.

- gridLineDashStyle: With this property, you can establish a line style as a dash into significant network lines.

- gridLineWidth: This property is for increasing and decreasing the width for the primary grid line for a chart. See Listing 6-2.

Listing 6-2. app.component.ts

```
yAxis: {
        gridLineDashStyle: 'dash',
        gridLineWidth: 2,
        gridLineColor: 'green'
        },
```

If you add the code in Listing 6-2 to the y-axis in a line chart and run it, you will get Figure 6-1.

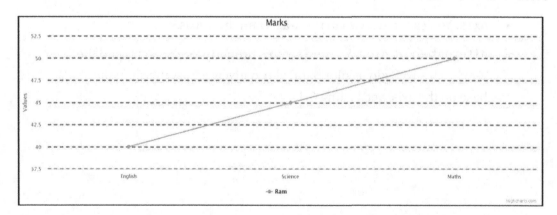

Figure 6-1. *Demo of gridLineDashStyle, gridLineWidth, and gridLineColor*

- tickWidth: This property is used to set the width for major ticks. You can set this for both the x-axis and the y-axis.

- tickPosition: By default, this property is outside. You can set it as inside, too; also, this will reflect in major ticks.

- tickColor: With this property, you can set a major tick color for the axis.

- tickLength: This will increase/decrease the length of main ticks in the form of a pixel. See Listing 6-3.

Listing 6-3. app.component.ts

```
xAxis: {
    categories:['English', 'Science', 'Maths'],
    tickWidth: 1,
    tickLength: 20,
    tickPosition:'inside',
    tickColor:'red',
},
```

If you add the above code to the x-axis, you will get the output shown in Figure 6-2.

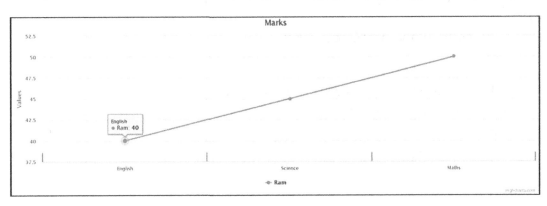

Figure 6-2. *Major tick-related properties for Highcharts*

- lineColor: This sets the axis line color for the chart.

- lineWidth: With this property, you can set the width of the axis line.

Applying a Dash Style Series to a Line Chart

Highcharts provides a dash style series for line charts. For this, you have to set series. dashStyle. You can set the value as LongDash, ShortDot, Dot, ShortDashDot, Dash, and DotDash. Copy the Listing 6-4 code into the dash-line-chart.component.ts file. See also the code in Listing 6-4.1.

Listing 6-4. dash-line-chart.component.ts

```typescript
import { Component, OnInit } from '@angular/core';
import * as Highcharts from 'highcharts';

interface ExtendedTitle extends Highcharts.TitleOptions {
  borderColor: string,
  borderRadius: number,
  borderWidth: number
}

@Component({
  selector: 'app-dash-line-chart',
  templateUrl: './dash-line-chart.component.html',
  styleUrls: ['./dash-line-chart.component.css']
})
export class DashLineChartComponent {

  title = 'myHighChartsApp';
  Highcharts: typeof Highcharts = Highcharts;
  chartOptions: Highcharts.Options = {
    chart: {
      type: 'line',
    },
    title: {
      text: 'Marks',
      backgroundColor: '#FCFFC5',
      borderColor: 'black',
      borderRadius: 10,
      borderWidth: 3
    } as ExtendedTitle,
```

```
  xAxis: {
    categories: ['English', 'Science', 'Maths'],
    tickWidth: 1,
    tickLength: 20,
    tickPosition: 'inside',
    tickColor: 'red',
  },
  series: [{
    type: 'line',
    name: 'Ram',
    data: [40, 45, 50],
    dashStyle: 'Dot'
  },
  {
    type: 'line',
    name: 'Jack',
    data: [44, 35, 30],
    dashStyle: 'ShortDot'
  },
  {
    name: 'John',
    type: 'line',
    data: [34, 25, 32],
    dashStyle: 'Dash'
  },
  {
    name: 'kate',
    type: 'line',
    data: [24, 38, 44],
    dashStyle: 'ShortDashDot'
  },
  ]
};
}
```

Listing 6-4.1. dash-line-chart.component.html

```
<div class="content" role="main">
    <highcharts-chart [Highcharts]="Highcharts" [options]="chartOptions"
        style="width: 100%; height: 400px; display: block;">
    </highcharts-chart>
</div>
```

Run the Listing 6-4 code and you will get the output seen in Figure 6-3.

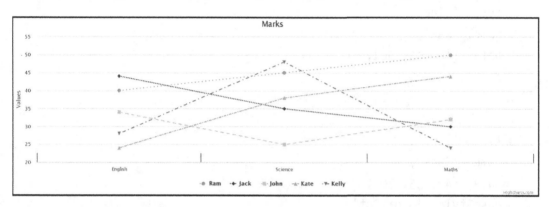

Figure 6-3. *dashStyle series in a line chart*

Combinations in Highcharts

Highcharts supports combinations, as in multiple charts in one place. Suppose you want to define a bar and spline in one chart to display a city's temperatures based on rainfall. You can do so very easily. Let's see one example of how you can set a combination using Highcharts and Angular.

In the upcoming example, you will plot a mutual fund's performance for the year against its benchmark index. To do so, you have to use a combination of charts. In this example, you'll use a column chart for the mutual fund scheme performance and a spline chart for the benchmark index. Look at Listing 6-5.

Listing 6-5. combination-chart.component.ts

```
series: [{
    name: 'Scheme',
    type: 'column',
```

```
    yAxis: 1,
    data: [7.43, 8.5, 5.4, 8.2, 8.97, 6.9, 7.6, 8.5, 8.4, 8.9,
    9.6, 10.4],
    tooltip: {
      valueSuffix: ' %'
    }
  }, {
    name: 'Benchmark',
    type: 'spline',
   data: [4.12, 3.9, 2.68, 3.5, 4.2, 2.5, 3.2, 6.5, 6.3, 7.3, 7.9, 7.6],
    tooltip: {
      valueSuffix: '%'
    }
  }],
```

In Listing 6-5, in one series array, you use the type property, so here you have two
series, one for Benchmark and one for Scheme performance. Remember that you should
have a good idea what type of series generation is required for that particular chart. Refer
to Chapter 4 where I describe different charting options in Highcharts. Listing 6-6 contains
the full code. You can copy this code into the combination-chart.component.ts file.

Listing 6-6. combination-chart.component.ts

```
import { Component, OnInit } from '@angular/core';
import * as Highcharts from 'highcharts';

interface ZoomExtend extends Highcharts.ChartOptions{
  zoomType : string;
}

@Component({
  selector: 'app-combination-chart',
  templateUrl: './combination-chart.component.html',
  styleUrls: ['./combination-chart.component.css']
})
export class CombinationChartComponent {
  title = 'myHighChartsApp';
  Highcharts: typeof Highcharts = Highcharts;
```

```
chartOptions: Highcharts.Options = {
  chart: {
    zoomType: 'xy'
  } as ZoomExtend,
  title: {
    text: 'IECE Digital Bluechip Fund (LargeCap Category)'
  },
  xAxis: [{
    categories: ['Jan', 'Feb', 'Mar', 'Apr', 'May', 'Jun',
      'Jul', 'Aug', 'Sep', 'Oct', 'Nov', 'Dec'],
  }],
  yAxis: [{
    labels: {
      format: '{value}%',
      style: {
        color: 'black',
      }
    },
    title: {
      text: 'Benchmark',
      style: {
        color: 'black',
      }
    }
  }, { // Secondary yAxis
    title: {
      text: 'Scheme',
      style: {
        color: 'blue',
      }
    },
    labels: {
      format: '{value} %',
      style: {
        color: 'green',
      }
    }
```

```
    },
    opposite: true
  }],
  tooltip: {
    shared: true
  },
  legend: {
    layout: 'vertical',
    align: 'left',
    x: 170,
    verticalAlign: 'top',
    y: 70,
    floating: true,
    backgroundColor:
      'gray'
  },
  series: [{
    name: 'Scheme',
    type: 'column',
    yAxis: 1,
    data: [7.43, 8.5, 5.4, 8.2, 8.97, 6.9, 7.6, 8.5, 8.4, 8.9,
    9.6, 10.4],
    tooltip: {
      valueSuffix: ' %'
    }
  }, {
    name: 'Benchmark',
    type: 'spline',
    data: [4.12, 3.9, 2.68, 3.5, 4.2, 2.5, 3.2, 6.5, 6.3, 7.3, 7.9, 7.6],
    tooltip: {
      valueSuffix: '%'
    }
  }],
  }
}
```

Now copy Listing 6-7's code into `app.component.html`.

Listing 6-7. combination-chart.component.html

```
<div class="content" role="main">
   <highcharts-chart [Highcharts]="Highcharts" [options]="chartOptions"
      style="width: 100%; height: 400px; display: block;">
   </highcharts-chart>
 </div>
<router-outlet></router-outlet>
```

Now, type ng serve into the terminal window of Visual Studio or type your URL in the browser. You will get the output seen in Figure 6-4.

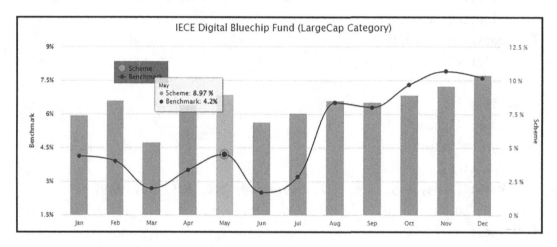

Figure 6-4. *Combination column/spline chart*

As you can see, there are two y-axes, one for Scheme and one for Benchmark.

Now let's see another example of a combination chart. This example is a combination of pie, spline, and column charts. In this chart, you will construct a graph for demonstrating the mobile operating systems used by different countries (Listing 6-8).

Listing 6-8. multi-chart.component.ts

```
series: [
    {
        type: 'column',
        name: 'India',
```

```
  data: [25, 55, 10, 5, 5],
  color:'LightSalmon',
},
{
  type: 'column',
  name: 'UK',
  data: [57, 30, 7, 3, 3],
  color:'olive',
},
{
  type: 'column',
  name: 'US',
  data: [50, 30, 15, 3, 2],
  color:'darkred'
},
{
  type: 'spline',
  name: 'Average',
  data: [44, 38.3, 10.67, 3.67, 3.34],
  marker: {
    lineWidth: 2,
    lineColor: 'green',
    fillColor: 'white',
  },
},
{
  type: 'pie', //total
  name: 'Total consumption',
  data: [
    {
      name: 'India',
      y: 100,
      color: 'LightSalmon',
    },
    {
```

```
            name: 'UK',
            y: 100,
            color: 'olive',
          },
          {
            name: 'US',
            y: 100,
            color: 'darkred',
          },
        ],
        center: [590, 80],
        size: 120,
        showInLegend: false,
        dataLabels: {
          enabled: false,
        },
      },
    ],
```

In this code, you have a series based on the chart type, so you must generate the series. This will construct a chart with column, spline, and pie. Listing 6-9 has the complete code, so copy it into the `multi-chart.component.ts` file.

Listing 6-9. multi-chart.component.ts

```typescript
import { Component, OnInit } from '@angular/core';
import * as Highcharts from 'highcharts';

interface ZoomExtend extends Highcharts.ChartOptions{
  zoomType : string;
}

interface ExtendedOptions extends Highcharts.Options
{
  labels : object;
}
@Component({
  selector: 'app-combination-chart',
```

```
    templateUrl: './combination-chart.component.html',
    styleUrls: ['./combination-chart.component.css']
})
export class CombinationChartComponent {
  title = 'myHighChartsApp';
  Highcharts: typeof Highcharts = Highcharts;
  chartOptions: ExtendedOptions = {
    chart: {
      zoomType: 'xy',
    } as ZoomExtend,
    title: {
      text: 'Mobile Operating System used by diffrent Countries in
      Percentage',
    },
    labels: {
      items: [
        {
          html: 'Total product used',
          style: {
            left: '550px',
            top: '18px',
            color: 'black',
          },
        },
      ],
    },
    xAxis: {
      categories: ['IOS', 'Android', 'Windows', 'Black Berry', 'Symbian'],
    },
    series: [
      {
        type: 'column',
        name: 'India',
        data: [25, 55, 10, 5, 5],
        color:'LightSalmon',
```

```
    },
    {
      type: 'column',
      name: 'UK',
      data: [57, 30, 7, 3, 3],
      color:'olive',
    },
    {
      type: 'column',
      name: 'US',
      data: [50, 30, 15, 3, 2],
      color:'darkred'
    },
    {
      type: 'spline',
      name: 'Average',
      data: [44, 38.3, 10.67, 3.67, 3.34],
      marker: {
        lineWidth: 2,
        lineColor: 'green',
        fillColor: 'white',
      },
    },
    {
      type: 'pie', //total
      name: 'Total consumption',
      data: [
        {
          name: 'India',
          y: 100,
          color: 'LightSalmon',
        },
        {
          name: 'UK',
          y: 100,
```

```
          color: 'olive',
        },
        {
          name: 'US',
          y: 100,
          color: 'darkred',
        },
      ],
      center: [590, 80],
      size: 120,
      showInLegend: false,
      dataLabels: {
        enabled: false,
      },
    },
  ],
};
}
```

Zoom Option in Highcharts

Note in Listing 6-9 the appearance of zoomType: 'xy'. You can set a chart.zoomType
property to the x-axis or y-axis, or if necessary you can arrange for the xy axis. You can
zoom by dragging your mouse pointer based on your setting in the form of x, y, or xy.

Once your zoom is done, on the top right-hand side of your chart area you will
automatically get one button as a Zoom Out option.

In label.item.style, you set style with the left and top properties; this is for
changing the position of the "Total product used" label in the chart area. It's the same as
for a pie chart; here the center and size properties set the position of the pie chart and
size of a pie.

Type ng serve into the terminal window of Visual Studio and you will get the output
shown in Figure 6-5.

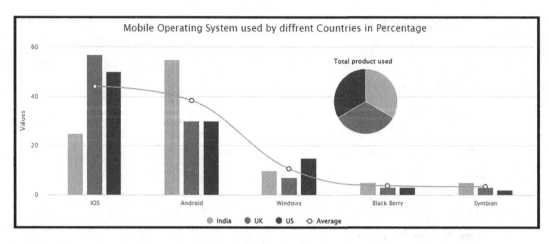

Figure 6-5. *Combination column/spline/pie chart*

Setting an Image in a Chart Area

You can set images to make your chart more interactive. In Highcharts, you have an option to arrange an image in the chart area.

For this, you must use the render method; with the use of the chart.renderer method, you can set an image. See Listing 6-10. This example is only a simple line chart with one image where you show the yearly temperature of a city in the summer season. On the left-hand side is an image of a sun.

Listing 6-10. image-chart.component.ts

```
chart: {
    events: {
      render: function () {
        var chart = this as ExtendedChart,
          renderer = chart.renderer,
          bg = chart.plotBackground;
        renderer
          .image(
        'https://www.highcharts.com/samples/graphics/sun.png',
          100,
          100,
          30,
```

```
            30
          )
         .add();
      },
    },
  }
```

Here you render the event method. In this method, you must extend
plotBackground: SVGAElement; here you use the ExtendedChart interface. You set a
variable as renderer = chart.renderer and then the renderer.image method is used
to set the path of the image, the image position, and the image size for the chart. This is
how to place an image in a chart. Listing 6-11 is the full code, so copy it into the image-
chart.component.ts file.

Listing 6-11. image-chart.component.ts

```
import { Component, OnInit } from '@angular/core';
import * as Highcharts from 'highcharts/highcharts';

// Introducing a custom property.
interface ExtendedChart extends Highcharts.Chart {
  plotBackground: SVGAElement;
}

@Component({
  selector: 'app-image-chart',
  templateUrl: './image-chart.component.html',
  styleUrls: ['./image-chart.component.css']
})
export class ImageChartComponent  {
  title = 'myHighChartsApp';
  Highcharts: typeof Highcharts = Highcharts;

  chartOptions: Highcharts.Options = {
    title: {
      text: 'Sample Count by Range',
    },
```

```
chart: {
  events: {
    render: function () {
      var chart = this as ExtendedChart,
        renderer = chart.renderer,
        bg = chart.plotBackground;
      renderer
        .image(
          'https://www.highcharts.com/samples/graphics/sun.png',
          100,
          100,
          30,
          30
        )
        .add();
    },
  },
},
xAxis: {
  categories: [
    '2013',
    '2014',
    '2015',
    '2016',
    '2017',
    '2018',
    '2019',
    '2020',
    '2021',
    '2022',
  ],
},
series: [
  {
    type: 'line',
```

```
    name: 'Temprature',
    data: [42.5, 41.3, 43.0, 44.0, 41.25, 42.52, 40.25, 44.5,
    48.0, 48.2],
    },
  ],
};
}
```

Type ng serve into the terminal window of Visual Studio. Once you run this code, you will get the output shown in Figure 6-6.

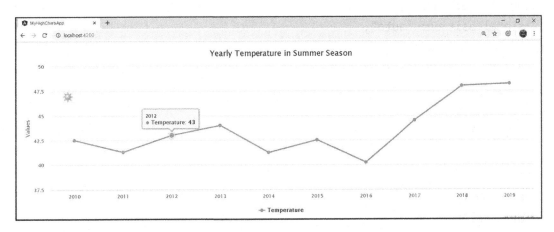

Figure 6-6. *Adding an image in a Highchart example*

3D Charts

Highcharts 3D provides 3D support to Highcharts. With this feature, you can develop an interactive chart. To work with a 3D chart, here are the required dependencies:

jQuery:

```
<script src="https://code.highcharts.com/highcharts-3d.js"></script>
```

Angular:

```
import * as Highcharts from 'highcharts';
import highcharts3D from 'highcharts/highcharts-3d';
highcharts3D(Highcharts);
```

To implement Highcharts 3D in code, see Listing 6-12.

Listing 6-12. app.component.ts

```
options3d:
      {
enabled: boolean,
alpha: number,
beta: number,
depth: number,
viewDistance: number,
axisLabelPosition: "auto",
fitToPlot: boolean,
frame: {
bottom: {
size: number,
color: 'color'
          },
back: {
size: number,
color: 'color'
          },
side: {
size: number,
color: 'color'
          },
      }
      }
```

You can use these properties based on your requirements:

- options3d: Required to develop a 3D chart; this is the leading property.

- enabled: This is a Boolean property. If true, you will see a 3D chart. If false, nothing will reflect.

- **alpha:** Number type of property; it will rotate in the bottom and top view level.

- **beta:** Number type of property; it will turn right and left.

- **depth:** This is for a total depth of chart.

- **viewDistance:** This defines how far viewers are from the chart.

- **frame:** This is for setting a chart from the bottom, back, and side.

Listing 6-13 is the full code, so copy it into app-chart3d.component.ts.

Listing 6-13. app-chart3d.component.ts

```
import { Component, OnInit } from '@angular/core';
import * as Highcharts from 'highcharts';
import highcharts3D from 'highcharts/highcharts-3d';
highcharts3D(Highcharts);

// Extending default chart type
interface ExtendedChart3dFrameOptions extends
Highcharts.Chart3dFrameOptions {
  side: object;
}

@Component({
  selector: 'app-chart3d',
  templateUrl: './chart3d.component.html',
  styleUrls: ['./chart3d.component.css']
})
export class Chart3dComponent {

  Highcharts: typeof Highcharts = Highcharts;

  chartOptions: Highcharts.Options = {
    chart: {
      options3d: {
        enabled: true,
        alpha: 10,
        beta: 45,
```

```
      depth: 150,
      viewDistance: 50,
      axisLabelPosition: 'auto',
      fitToPlot: true,
      frame: {
        bottom: {
          size: 10,
          color: 'orange',
        },
        back: {
          size: 10,
          color: 'orange',
        },
        side: {
          size: 10,
          color: 'orange',
        },
      } as ExtendedChart3dFrameOptions,
    },
  },
  title: {
    text: 'Real Time Data Example',
  },
  xAxis: {
    categories: ['English', 'Maths', 'Science'],
  },
  yAxis: {
    title: {
      text: 'Marks',
    },
  },
  plotOptions: {
    column: {
      depth: 65,
    },
```

```
  },
  series: [
    {
      type: 'column',
      data: [35, 49, 42],
    },
  ],
};
}
```

Type ng serve into a terminal window of Visual Studio and you will get the output shown in Figure 6-7.

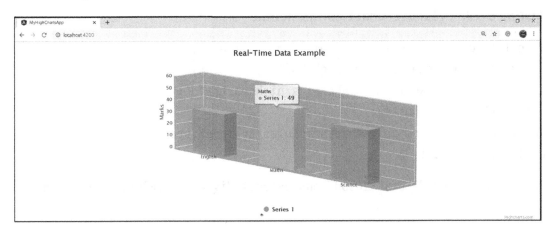

Figure 6-7. *Highcharts 3D example for a column type chart*

Cylinder Chart

A cylinder chart is another type of 3D chart. If you want to implement a cylinder, the following dependencies are required:

jQuery:

```
<script src="https://code.highcharts.com/highcharts-3d.js"></script>
<script src="https://code.highcharts.com/modules/cylinder.js"></script>
```

Angular:

```
import * as Highcharts from 'highcharts';
import highcharts3D from 'highcharts/highcharts-3d';
highcharts3D(Highcharts);
import cylinder from 'highcharts/modules/cylinder.src'
cylinder(Highcharts);
```

For implementing a cylinder chart, the type should be cylinder. You must add the dependency as per your JavaScript framework.

Copy Listing 6-14's code into cylinder-chart.component.ts to generate a cylinder chart.

Listing 6-14. cylinder-chart.component.ts

```
import { Component, OnInit } from '@angular/core';
import * as Highcharts from 'highcharts';
import highcharts3D from 'highcharts/highcharts-3d';
highcharts3D(Highcharts);
import cylinder from 'highcharts/modules/cylinder.src'
cylinder(Highcharts);

interface ExtendedPlotSeriesOptions extends Highcharts.PlotSeriesOptions {
  depth: any;
}

@Component({
  selector: 'app-cylider-chart',
  templateUrl: './cylider-chart.component.html',
  styleUrls: ['./cylider-chart.component.css']
})
export class CyliderChartComponent {
  title = 'myHighChartsApp';
  Highcharts: typeof Highcharts = Highcharts;
  chartOptions: Highcharts.Options = {
    chart: {
      renderTo: 'container',
      type: 'cylinder',
```

```
      options3d:
      {
        enabled: true,
        beta: 15,
        alpha: 15,
        viewDistance: 15,
        depth: 50,
      }
    },
    title: {
      text: 'Real Time Data Example'
    },
    xAxis: {
      categories: ['English', 'Maths', 'Science']
    },
    yAxis: {
      title: {
        text: 'Marks'
      },
    },
    plotOptions: {
      series: {
        depth: 25,
        colorByPoint: true
      } as ExtendedPlotSeriesOptions
    },
    series: [{
      type: 'cylinder',
      data: [35, 49, 42]
    }],
  }
}
```

Now type ng serve and you will get the output shown in Figure 6-8.

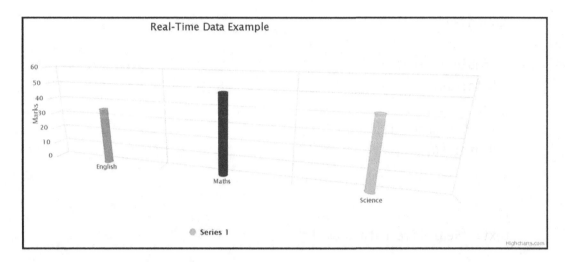

Figure 6-8. *Cylinder chart example*

Funnel 3D

The funnel 3D chart type is another type used for 3D charting in Highcharts. A funnel chart is used to display different stages in a business process; the completed process is on the top and the pending process is on the bottom.

To implement the funnel 3D chart, the following dependencies are required:

jQuery:

```
<script src="https://code.highcharts.com/highcharts-3d.js"></script>
<script src="https://code.highcharts.com/modules/cylinder.js"></script>
<script src="https://code.highcharts.com/modules/funnel3d.js"></script>
```

Angular:

```
import * as Highcharts from 'highcharts/highcharts';
import highcharts3D from 'highcharts/highcharts-3d';
highcharts3D(Highcharts);
import cylinder from 'highcharts/modules/cylinder'
cylinder(Highcharts);
import funnel3d from 'highcharts/modules/funnel3d';
funnel3d(Highcharts);
```

To create a funnel 3D chart, the chart `type` should be `funnel3d`, and the next step should be to define the series. See Listing 6-15.

Listing 6-15. funnel-chart.component.ts

```
series: [{
    type: 'funnel3d',
    name: 'Customers',
    data: [
      ['Customer visits Website totally', 8000],
      ['App Downloads', 5150],
      ['Requested price list', 2000],
      ['Proposal sent', 1600],
    ]
  }],
```

Listing 6-15 shows labels and values for the data series for the funnel. Next, you require `plotOptions`; see Listing 6-16.

Listing 6-16. funnel-chart.component.ts

```
plotOptions: {
    series: {
      dataLabels: {
        enabled: true,
        format: '<b>{point.name}</b> ({point.y:,.0f})',
        allowOverlap: true,
      },
      height: '50%',
      width: '40%',
      neckWidth: '15%',
      neckHeight: '15%',
    } as ExtendPlotSeriesOptions
  },
```

In `plotOptions`, you can set `height`, `width`, and format-related settings for `funnel3d`. Listing 6-17 is the full code to generate `funnel3d`, so copy this code into the `app.components.ts` file.

Listing 6-17. funnel-chart.component.ts

```
import { Component, OnInit } from '@angular/core';
import * as Highcharts from 'highcharts/highcharts';
import highcharts3D from 'highcharts/highcharts-3d';
highcharts3D(Highcharts);
import cylinder from 'highcharts/modules/cylinder'
cylinder(Highcharts);
import funnel3d from 'highcharts/modules/funnel3d';
funnel3d(Highcharts);

interface ExtendPlotSeriesOptions extends Highcharts.PlotSeriesOptions{
  height:string;
}

@Component({
  selector: 'app-funnel-chart',
  templateUrl: './funnel-chart.component.html',
  styleUrls: ['./funnel-chart.component.css']
})
export class FunnelChartComponent {
  Highcharts: typeof Highcharts = Highcharts;
  chartOptions: Highcharts.Options = {
    title: {
      text: 'Highcharts Funnel3D Chart'
    },
    chart: {
      renderTo: 'container',
      type: 'funnel3d',
      options3d: {
        enabled: true,
        alpha: 10,
        depth: 50,
        viewDistance: 50
      }
    },
```

```
  series: [{
    type: 'funnel3d',
    name: 'Customers',
    data: [
      ['Customer visits Website totally', 8000],
      ['App Downloads', 5150],
      ['Requested price list', 2000],
      ['Proposal sent', 1600],
    ]
  }],
  plotOptions: {
    series: {
      dataLabels: {
        enabled: true,
        format: '<b>{point.name}</b> ({point.y:,.0f})',
        allowOverlap: true,
      },
      height: '50%',
      width: '40%',
      neckWidth: '15%',
      neckHeight: '15%',
    } as ExtendPlotSeriesOptions
  },
 }
}
```

Type ng serve and press Enter. You will get the output shown in Figure 6-9.

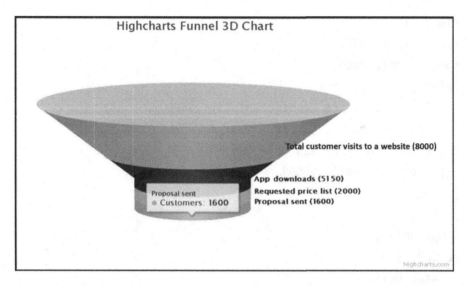

Figure 6-9. *Funnel 3D chart*

Pyramid 3D

A pyramid chart is a triangle-based chart. The triangle has sections, and these sections work top to bottom. This type of chart is mostly used to show hierarchy, priorities, steps, or processes.

To work on a pyramid 3D chart, the following dependencies are required:

jQuery:

```
<script src="https://code.highcharts.com/highcharts.js"></script>
<script src="https://code.highcharts.com/highcharts-3d.js"></script>
<script src="https://code.highcharts.com/modules/cylinder.js"></script>
<script src="https://code.highcharts.com/modules/funnel3d.js"></script>
<script src="https://code.highcharts.com/modules/pyramid3d.js"></script>
```

Angular:

```
import { Component, OnInit } from '@angular/core';
import * as Highcharts from 'highcharts';
import highcharts3D from 'highcharts/highcharts-3d';
highcharts3D(Highcharts);
import cylinder from 'highcharts/modules/cylinder';
cylinder(Highcharts);
```

180

```
import funnel3d from 'highcharts/modules/funnel3d';
funnel3d(Highcharts);
import pyramid3d from 'highcharts/modules/pyramid3d';
pyramid3d(Highcharts);
```

This demo is the same as the one for the funnel3d. A 3D pyramid works top to bottom. Copy Listing 6-18's code into pyramid3d-chart.component.ts.

Listing 6-18. pyramid3d-chart.component.ts

```
import { Component, OnInit } from '@angular/core';
import * as Highcharts from 'highcharts';
import highcharts3D from 'highcharts/highcharts-3d';
highcharts3D(Highcharts);
import cylinder from 'highcharts/modules/cylinder';
cylinder(Highcharts);
import funnel3d from 'highcharts/modules/funnel3d';
funnel3d(Highcharts);
import pyramid3d from 'highcharts/modules/pyramid3d';
pyramid3d(Highcharts);

interface ExtendPlotSeriesOptions extends Highcharts.PlotSeriesOptions{
  height:string;
}
@Component({
  selector: 'app-pyramid3d-chart',
  templateUrl: './pyramid3d-chart.component.html',
  styleUrls: ['./pyramid3d-chart.component.css']
})
export class Pyramid3dChartComponent {
  Highcharts: typeof Highcharts = Highcharts;
  chartOptions: Highcharts.Options = {
    title: {
      text: 'Pyramid3D Chart Demo'
    },
    chart: {
      renderTo: 'container',
```

181

```
      type: 'pyramid3d',
      options3d: {
        enabled: true,
        alpha: 10,
        depth: 50,
        viewDistance: 50
      }
    },
    series: [{
      type: 'pyramid3d',
      name: 'Customers',
      data: [
        ['Customer visits Website totally', 8000],
        ['App Downloads', 5150],
        ['Requested price list', 2000],
        ['Proposal sent', 1600],
      ]
    }],
    plotOptions: {
      series: {
        dataLabels: {
          enabled: true,
          format: '<b>{point.name}</b> ({point.y:,.0f})',
          allowOverlap: true,
        },
        width: '40%',
        height: '60%',
      }as ExtendPlotSeriesOptions
    },
  }
}
```

Once you run this code, you will get the output shown in Figure 6-10.

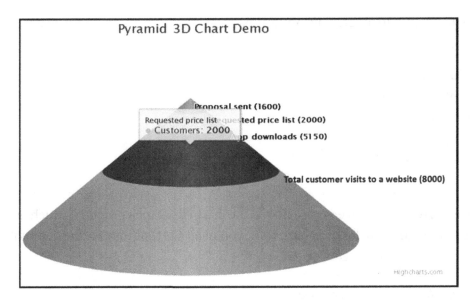

Figure 6-10. Pyramid 3D chart

Pie 3D Chart

With the pie 3D chart, you can add 3D features very easily. Here the chart type is pie. And you must add the following dependencies:

jQuery:

```
<script src="https://code.highcharts.com/highcharts.js"></script>
<script src="https://code.highcharts.com/highcharts-3d.js"></script>
```

Angular:

```
import * as Highcharts from 'highcharts/highcharts';
import highcharts3D from 'highcharts/highcharts-3d';
highcharts3D(Highcharts);
```

Next, you have to set options3d and plotOptions. See Listing 6-19.

Listing 6-19. pie3d-chart.component.ts

```
chart: {
type: 'pie',
      options3d: {
enabled: true,
alpha: 65,
      }
    },
```

Here `options3d.enabled` is `true`. Note the use of the `alpha` property, which is required for rotating angles of a chart. Next, you need `plotOptions` for the depth of the chart for 3D; see Listing 6-20.

Listing 6-20. app.component.ts

```
plotOptions: {
pie: {
allowPointSelect: true,
cursor: 'pointer',
depth: 65,
dataLabels: {
enabled: true,
format: '<b>{point.name}</b>: {point.percentage:.1f} %'
      }
    }
  },
```

Paste Listing 6-21's complete code into the `pie3d-chart.component.ts` file.

Listing 6-21. pie3d-chart.component.ts

```
import { Component, OnInit } from '@angular/core';
import * as Highcharts from 'highcharts/highcharts';
import highcharts3D from 'highcharts/highcharts-3d';
highcharts3D(Highcharts);
```

```
@Component({
  selector: 'app-pie3d-chart',
  templateUrl: './pie3d-chart.component.html',
  styleUrls: ['./pie3d-chart.component.css']
})
export class Pie3dChartComponent {
  Highcharts: typeof Highcharts = Highcharts;
  chartOptions: Highcharts.Options = {
    chart: {
      type: 'pie',
      options3d: {
        enabled: true,
        alpha: 65,
      }
    },
    plotOptions: {
      pie: {
        allowPointSelect: true,
        cursor: 'pointer',
        depth: 65,
        dataLabels: {
          enabled: true,
        format: '<b>{point.name}</b>: {point.percentage:.1f} %'
        }
      }
    },
    title: {
     text: 'Programming Languages used by developers worldwide'
    },
    tooltip: {
    pointFormat: '{series.name}: <b>{point.percentage:.1f}%</b>'
    },
    series: [{
      name: 'Uses',
      colorByPoint: true,
```

```
    type: 'pie',
    data: [{
      name: 'C#',
      y: 55,
      sliced: true,
      selected: true
    }, {
      name: 'VB',
      y: 25
    }, {
      name: 'J#',
      y: 10
    }, {
      name: 'VC++',
      y: 10
    }]
  }]
};
}
```

Run the Listing 6-21 code and you will get the output shown in Figure 6-11.

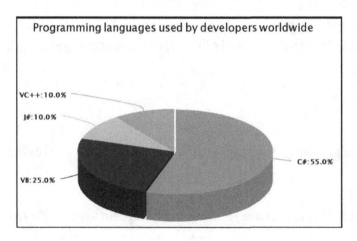

Figure 6-11. *3D pie chart*

You can convert the same chart into a donut chart with the use of plotOptions.pie. innersize: number. See Listing 6-22.

Listing 6-22. app.component.ts

```
plotOptions: {
pie: {
innerSize: 100,
    }
  }
```

If you add the code in Listing 6-22 to `app.component.ts` and run it, you will get the output shown in Figure 6-12.

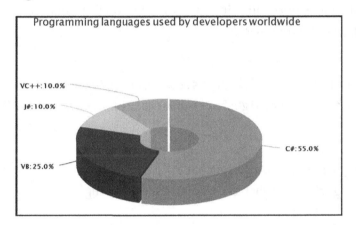

Figure 6-12. *3D donut chart demo*

Exporting and Printing Charts

Highcharts also provide export and print features, so a user can print and download charts easily in the PNG, JPEG, PDF, XLS, CSV, and SVG formats. For exporting and printing, Highcharts provides different dependencies.

- `Exporting.js`: This js dependency provides the following options:
  - View in full screen
  - Print chart
  - Download PNG image
  - Download JPEG
  - Download PDF
  - Download SVG vector

- Export-data.js: If you want to add more options related to exporting to CSV and XLS, this dependency is required, but you have to add Exporting.js with it. Export-data.js adds the following options:

  - Download CSV

  - Download XLS

  - View in data table

  - Open in Highcharts cloud

If you want to add export and print functionality, you must add these dependencies based on your JavaScript framework:

jQuery:

```
<script src="https://code.highcharts.com/modules/exporting.js"></script>
<script src="https://code.highcharts.com/modules/export-data.js"></script>
```

Angular:

```
import * as Highcharts from "highcharts";
import exporting from 'highcharts/modules/exporting';
exporting(Highcharts);
```

Once you add the dependency to your code, you will automatically get the right-hand menu bar. If you click this menu, you will get the export and print features. See Figure 6-13.

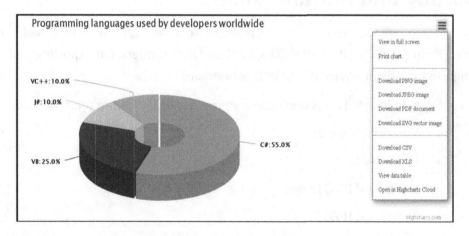

Figure 6-13. *Export and print options in Highcharts*

Additional Chart Features

This section covers new charts provided by Highcharts.

Radar Chart

A radar chart is useful for providing multivariate data, data you get in two dimensional or more quantitative variables. Radar charts are helpful for showing a comparison of data or if you want to show ratings for analyzing a particular product by its features.

In this demo, you will show a comparison of two mobile features so people can analyze which one is best, based on functionality.

If you want to create a radar polar chart using Highcharts, the first step is to set `chart.polar: true`. In `chart.type`, you can set `area`, `line`, `spline`, and `columns`. To develop polar radar charts, the following dependencies are required:

jQuery:

```
<script src="http://code.highcharts.com/highcharts.js"></script>
<script src="http://code.highcharts.com/highcharts-more.js"></script>
```

Angular:

```
import { Component } from '@angular/core';
import * as Highcharts from 'highcharts';
import More from 'highcharts/highcharts-more';
More(Highcharts);
```

Now copy Listing 6-23's code into the `radar-chart.component.ts` file.

Listing 6-23. radar-chart.component.ts

```
import { Component, OnInit } from '@angular/core';
import * as Highcharts from 'highcharts';
import More from 'highcharts/highcharts-more';
More(Highcharts);

@Component({
  selector: 'app-radar-chart',
  templateUrl: './radar-chart.component.html',
```

```
  styleUrls: ['./radar-chart.component.css']
})
export class RadarChartComponent {
  title = 'myHighChartsApp';
  Highcharts: typeof Highcharts = Highcharts;
  chartOptions: Highcharts.Options = {
    chart: {
      polar: true,
      type: 'line',
    },
    pane: {
      size: '80%'
    },
    title: {
      text: 'Comparison of Mobile Phones',
    },
    tooltip: {
      shared: true,
      pointFormat: '<span style="color:{series.color}">{series.name}:
      <b>{point.y:,.0f}</b><br/>'
    },
    xAxis: {
      categories: ['Camera', 'Battery', 'Brand', 'Memory',
        'Display', 'Durable'],
      tickmarkPlacement: 'on',
      lineWidth: 0
    },
    yAxis: {
      gridLineInterpolation: 'polygon',
      lineWidth: 0,
      min: 0
    },
    legend: {
      align: 'left',
      verticalAlign: 'middle'
```

```
    },
    series: [{
      type: 'line',
      name: 'VG Mobiles',
      data: [5, 4, 4, 3, 2, 3],
      pointPlacement: 'on'
    }, {
      name: 'Kiara Mobiles',
      type: 'line',
      data: [4, 3, 5, 1, 5, 4],
      pointPlacement: 'on'
    }],
  };
}
```

Run Listing 6-23's code and you will get the output shown in Figure 6-14.

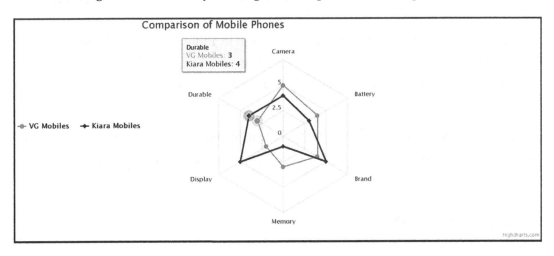

Figure 6-14. *Radar chart demo*

Pareto Chart

A Pareto chart is a combination of a line and bar graph, where values are defined in the form of descending order through bars and the cumulative total comes as a line. First of all, you must understand how Pareto works. Table 6-1 describes hair loss reasons for men.

Table 6-1. *Hair Loss Reasons for Men*

Hair Loss Reason	Frequency	Cumulative Frequency	Percentage
Genetics	50	50	57.47%
Cosmetic damage	15	65	74.71%
Stress	11	76	87.35%
Smoking	6	82	94.25%
Vitamin deficiency	3	85	97.70%
Infections	2	87	100%
Total	87		

Table 6-1 shows hair loss reason and frequency. The cumulative frequency is based on the next value total. For example, genetics + cosmetic damage = cumulative frequency. Based on totality, you create a percentage, and the percentage part comes into the Pareto section.

For this example, you'll convert the information in Table 6-1 into Highcharts with the Pareto chart.

To generate a Pareto chart, the following dependencies are required:

jQuery:

```
<script src="https://code.highcharts.com/highcharts.js"></script>
<script src="https://code.highcharts.com/modules/pareto.js"></script>
```

Angular:

```
import { Component, OnInit } from '@angular/core';
import * as Highcharts from "highcharts";
import Pareto from 'highcharts/modules/pareto';
Pareto(Highcharts);
```

Next, you must set the y-axis. See Listing 6-24.

Listing 6-24. pareto-chart.component.ts

```
yAxis: [{
title: {
text: ''
     }
   }, {
title: {
text: ''
     },
minPadding: 0,
maxPadding: 0,
max: 100,
min: 0,
opposite: true,
labels: {
format: "{value}%"
     }
   }],
```

In Listing 6-24, you have set a min and max property for Percentage. In the next part, you have a series for both columns and Pareto. See Listing 6-25.

Listing 6-25. pareto-chart.component.ts

```
series: [{
type: 'pareto',
name: 'Pareto',
yAxis: 1, //number of declared yaxis
baseSeries: 1 //index of column series
   },
{
name: 'Frequency',
type: 'column',
data: [50, 15, 11, 6, 3, 2],
color: '#FF0000'
   }]
```

Listing 6-26 is the complete code for generating the Pareto chart, so copy this code into the pareto-chart.component.ts file.

Listing 6-26. pareto-chart.component.ts

```
import { Component, OnInit } from '@angular/core';
import * as Highcharts from "highcharts";
import Pareto from 'highcharts/modules/pareto';
Pareto(Highcharts);

@Component({
  selector: 'app-pareto-chart',
  templateUrl: './pareto-chart.component.html',
  styleUrls: ['./pareto-chart.component.css']
})
export class ParetoChartComponent {
  title = 'myHighChartsApp';
  Highcharts: typeof Highcharts = Highcharts;
  chartOptions: Highcharts.Options = {
    chart: {
      type: 'column'
    },
    title: {
      text: 'Haifall Reasons for Men',
    },
    tooltip: {
      shared: true,
    },
    xAxis: {
      categories: [
        'Genetically',
        'Cosmetic damage',
        'Stress',
        'Smoke',
        'Vitamin Defficiency',
        'Infections',
      ],
```

```
    },
    yAxis: [{
      title: {
        text: ''
      }
    }, {
      title: {
        text: ''
      },
      minPadding: 0,
      maxPadding: 0,
      max: 100,
      min: 0,
      opposite: true,
      labels: {
        format: "{value}%"
      }
    }],
    series: [{
      type: 'pareto',
      name: 'Pareto',
      yAxis: 1, //number of declared yAxis
      baseSeries: 1 //index of column series
    }, {
      name: 'Frequency',
      type: 'column',
      data: [50, 15, 11, 6, 3, 2],
      color: '#FF0000'
    }]
  };
}
```

Run Listing 6-26's code and you will get the output shown in Figure 6-15.

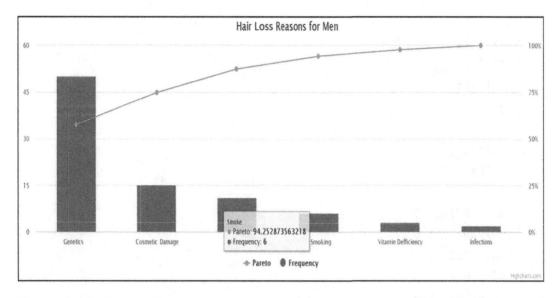

Figure 6-15. *Pareto Chart*

Bell Curve Chart

A bell curve chart is used for distribution of variables. Considering a normal distribution with a bell shape line, the highest point in the curve represents the most probable event in the series of data.

To generate a bell curve using Highcharts, the following dependencies are required:

jQuery:

```
<script src="https://code.highcharts.com/highcharts.js"></script>
<script src="https://code.highcharts.com/modules/histogram-bellcurve.js">
</script>
```

Angular:

```
import * as Highcharts from 'highcharts';
import Bellcurve from 'highcharts/modules/histogram-bellcurve';
Bellcurve(Highcharts);
```

In the next step, the chart `type` should be `bellcurve`, and the `baseSeries` you can define in the form of id or index.

Copy Listing 6-27's code into the `app.component.ts` file to generate the bell curve.

Listing 6-27. app.component.ts

```
import { Component } from '@angular/core';
import * as Highcharts from 'highcharts';
import Bellcurve from 'highcharts/modules/histogram-bellcurve';
Bellcurve(Highcharts);

@Component({
  selector: 'app-root',
templateUrl: './app.component.html',
styleUrls: ['./app.component.css']
})

export class AppComponent {
  title = 'myHighChartsApp';
  Highcharts: typeof Highcharts = Highcharts;
chartOptions: Highcharts.Options = {
  title: {
      text: 'Bell Curve'
    },
xAxis: [{
      title: { text: 'Data' },
    }, {
      title: { text: 'Bell Curve' },
      opposite: true
    }],
yAxis: [{
      title: { text: 'Data' }
    }, {
      title: { text: 'Bell Curve' },
      opposite: true
    }],
    series: [{
      name: 'Bell Curve',
      type: 'bellcurve',
xAxis: 1,
yAxis: 1,
```

```
baseSeries: 'series1',
zIndex: -1
        },
        {
            name: 'Data',
            type: 'scatter',
            data: [5, 5.2, 5.4, 5.5, 5.6, 5.9, 6],
            visible: true,
            id: 'series1',
        }]
    };
}
```

If you run the code in Listing 6-27, you will get the output shown in Figure 6-16.

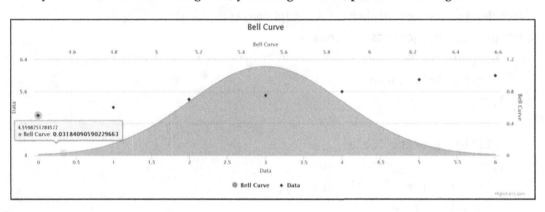

Figure 6-16. *Bell curve demo*

Organization Chart

An organization chart is a flow diagram chart that shows the complete hierarchy of an organization, which is how each individual is connected from top to bottom.

Organization charts connect from top to bottom with nodes, where each rank is connected with label. Here the chart type will be organization. Then you must define keys in [form and to]. Then you required data, where you will define your labels in the form of an array.

As you can see in the code, there is a levels section which is also array-based collection. Here you can set levels from top to bottom. You can define a level in the form of 0, 1, 2 and set its color. There is one more property called datalabels; here you can set color.

```
levels: [
        {
          level: 0,
          color: 'green',
dataLabels: {
            color: 'black',
          },
          height: 25,
        } as ExtendedPlotOrganizationLevelsOptions,
        {
          level: 1,
          color: 'orange',
dataLabels: {
            color: 'black',
          },
          height: 25,
        },
        {
          level: 2,
          color: '#980104',
        },
      ]
```

Then you must set the nodes property. This is an array property that is helpful for connecting layers from top to bottom.

```
nodes: [
        {
          id: 'Shareholders',
        },
        {
          id: 'Board',
```

```
      },
      {
        id: 'CEO',
        title: 'CEO',
        name: 'Sourabh Mishra',
        image:
'https://m.media-amazon.com/images/S/amzn-author-media-prod/5khlg
2dgom6plqp7ptfumc8n4s._SX450_.jpg',
      },
      {
        id: 'CTO',
        title: 'CTO',
        name: 'Andre P.',
        color: '#007ad0',
      },
      {
        id: 'HR',
        title: 'CFO',
        name: 'VB Jain',
        color: '#007ad0',
      },
      {
        id: 'Product',
        name: 'Database Administrator',
      },
    ],
```

This example is the IECE Digital Organization Chart in the form of top to bottom (stockholders, board, CEO, CTO, CFO, and so on).

If you want to develop an organization chart, the following dependencies are required:

jQuery:

```
<script src="https://code.highcharts.com/highcharts.js"></script>
<script src="https://code.highcharts.com/modules/sankey.js"></script>
<script src="https://code.highcharts.com/modules/organization.js"></script>
<script src="https://code.highcharts.com/modules/accessibility.js"></script>
```

Angular:

```
import * as Highcharts from 'highcharts/highcharts';
import Sankey from 'highcharts/modules/sankey';
import Organization from 'highcharts/modules/organization';
import Accessability from 'highcharts/modules/accessibility';
Sankey(Highcharts);
Organization(Highcharts);
Accessability(Highcharts);
```

For complete code understanding, copy the code in Listing 6-28 into the organization-chart.component.ts file.

Listing 6-28. organization-chart.component.ts

```
import { Component, OnInit } from '@angular/core';
import * as Highcharts from 'highcharts/highcharts';
import Sankey from 'highcharts/modules/sankey';
import Organization from 'highcharts/modules/organization';
import Accessability from 'highcharts/modules/accessibility';
Sankey(Highcharts);
Organization(Highcharts);
Accessability(Highcharts);

// Introducing a custom property.
interface ExtendedPoint extends Highcharts.Point {
toNode: {
    name: String;
    id: String;
  };
fromNode: {
    id: String;
  };
}
interface ExtendedPlotOrganizationLevelsOptions
  extends Highcharts.PlotOrganizationLevelsOptions {
  height: Number;
}
```

```
@Component({
  selector: 'app-organisation-chart',
templateUrl: './organisation-chart.component.html',
styleUrls: ['./organisation-chart.component.css']
})
export class OrganisationChartComponent {
  Highcharts: typeof Highcharts = Highcharts;
chartOptions: Highcharts.Options = {
    chart: {
      height: 600,
      inverted: true,
    },
    title: {
      text: 'IECE Digital Organisation Chart',
    },
  series: [
      {
        type: 'organization',
        name: 'IECE',
        keys: ['from', 'to'],
        data: [
          ['Stackholders', 'Board'],
          ['Board', 'CEO'],
          ['CEO', 'CTO'],
          ['CEO', 'HR'],
          ['CTO', 'Product'],
          ['CTO', 'Web'],
          ['HR', 'Market'],
          ['HR', 'Market'],
          ['CTO', 'Market'],
        ] as any,
        levels: [
          {
            level: 0,
```

```
                color: 'green',
dataLabels: {
                    color: 'black',
                },
                height: 25,
            } as ExtendedPlotOrganizationLevelsOptions,
            {
                level: 1,
                color: 'orange',
dataLabels: {
                    color: 'black',
                },
                height: 25,
            },
            {
                level: 2,
                color: '#980104',
            },
            {
                level: 4,
                color: '#359154',
            },
        ],
        nodes: [
            {
                id: 'Shareholders',
            },
            {
                id: 'Board',
            },
            {
                id: 'CEO',
                title: 'CEO',
                name: 'Sourabh Mishra',
```

```
            image:
'https://m.media-amazon.com/images/S/amzn-author-media-prod/5khlg2dgom6plqp
7ptfumc8n4s._SX450_.jpg',
          },
          {
            id: 'CTO',
            title: 'CTO',
            name: 'Andre P.',
            color: '#007ad0',
          },
          {
            id: 'HR',
            title: 'CFO',
            name: 'VB Jain',
            color: '#007ad0',
          },
          {
            id: 'Product',
            name: 'Database Administrator',
          },
          {
            id: 'Web',
            name: 'Web devs, sys admin',
          },
          {
            id: 'Market',
            name: 'Marketing team',
            column: 5,
          },
        ],
colorByPoint: false,
        color: '#007ad0',
dataLabels: {
        color: 'white',
        },
```

```
borderColor: 'white',
nodeWidth: 65,
        },
    ],
    tooltip: {
      outside: true,
    },
  };
}
```

Now it's time to add code for the `.html` file, so add the code in Listing 6-29 to `organization-chart.component.html`.

Listing 6-29. organization-chart.component.html

```
<highcharts-chart [Highcharts]="Highcharts" [options]="chartOptions">
</highcharts-chart>
```

Run this code using `ng serve` and you will get the output shown in Figure 6-17.

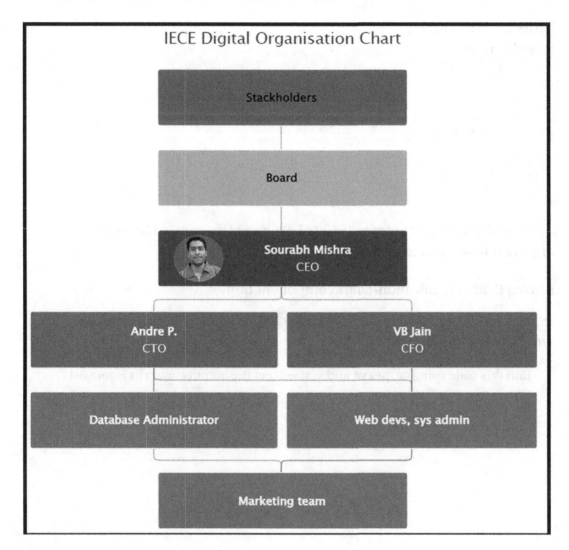

Figure 6-17. *Organization chart*

Timeline Chart

The timeline chart is designed to show a journey over time. Here you can define essential events in the form of a vertical or horizontal line. For each event, you can set a description for the event so via a tooltip the user can get details about the event. If you want to perform a timeline chart using Highcharts, the following dependencies are required:

jQuery:

```
<script src="https://code.highcharts.com/highcharts.js"></script>
<script src="https://code.highcharts.com/modules/timeline.js"></script>
```

Angular:

```
import * as Highcharts from 'highcharts';
import TimeLine from 'highcharts/modules/timeline';
TimeLine(Highcharts);
```

Now copy Listing 6-30's code into timelineSeries-Chart.component.ts.

Listing 6-30. timelineseries-Chart.component.ts

```
import { Component, OnInit } from '@angular/core';
import * as Highcharts from 'highcharts';
import TimeLine from 'highcharts/modules/timeline';
TimeLine(Highcharts);

@Component({
  selector: 'app-timeline-series-chart',
  templateUrl: './timeline-series-chart.component.html',
  styleUrls: ['./timeline-series-chart.component.css']
})
export class TimelineSeriesChartComponent  {
  Highcharts: typeof Highcharts = Highcharts;

  chartOptions: Highcharts.Options = {
    chart: {
      type: 'timeline',
      inverted: true
    },
    yAxis: {
      visible: false
    },
    title: {
      text: 'Journey of IECE Group'
    },
```

```
  series: [{
    type: 'timeline',
    dataLabels: {
      connectorColor: 'black',
      connectorWidth: 3
    },
    data: [{
      name: 'Company Founded',
      label: '1975: Institute Of Electronics Born',
      description: 'In the year 1975, Institute of Electronics found to
      provide trainings for Electrical/Electronics Engineers'
    }, {
      name: 'IECE founded',
      label: '1999: Company Expend into Computer Education',
      description: 'With new Name IECE, company starts provide training
      into Computer Scienece Students as well'
    }, {
      name: 'IECE Inventory Controller Launch',
      label: '2003: First Software Launch',
      description: '4th December 2003, First Software launch with name
      IECE Inventory Controller'
    }, {
      name: 'IECE Digital launch',
      label: '2018: IECE Digital founded',
      description: 'IECE Digital launch, to provide world class animation
      and VFX.'
    }],
  }]
};
}
```

In Listing 6-30, the chart type is timeline. On the next line is a property called inverted: true, and this means you can see your timeline in vertical mode. If you want to develop in horizontal mode, make it false. Next in the series section is a property called dataLabels; here you can set colors and width for the connector lines for the labels. Once you run the above code, you will get the output shown in Figure 6-18.

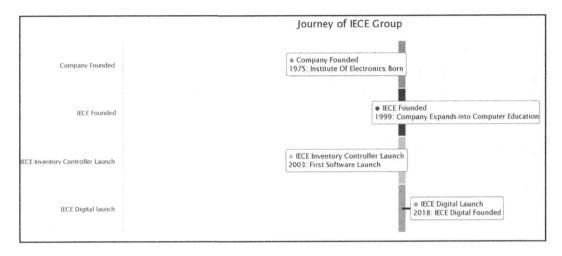

Figure 6-18. *A timeline chart demo using Highcharts*

Gantt Chart

A Gantt chart is used to demonstrate project progress. Henry Gantt introduced the Gantt chart. This type of chart also shows project activities and current schedule status relationships. In a Gantt chart, the vertical axis can define the task to perform and the horizontal axis can represent the time interval and progress.

If you want to develop a Gantt chart, the following dependencies are required:

jQuery:

```
<script src="https://code.highcharts.com/highcharts.js"></script>
<script src="https://code.highcharts.com/gantt/highcharts-gantt.
js"></script>
```

Angular:

```
import { Component } from '@angular/core';
import * as Highcharts from 'highcharts';
import GanttModule from 'highcharts/modules/gantt';
GanttModule(Highcharts);
```

Listing 6-31 has the code to show the progress of a software development project with the use of a Gantt chart. Copy Listing 6-31's code into the `gantt-chart.component.ts` file.

Listing 6-31. gantt-chart.component.ts

```
import { Component } from '@angular/core';
import * as Highcharts from 'highcharts';
import GanttModule from 'highcharts/modules/gantt';
GanttModule(Highcharts);

Highcharts.setOptions({
title: {
style: {
color: 'blue'
    }
  },
legend: {
enabled: false
  }
});

@Component({
  selector: 'app-gantt-chart',
  templateUrl: './gantt-chart.component.html',
  styleUrls: ['./gantt-chart.component.css']
})
export class GanttChartComponent {
  Highcharts: typeof Highcharts = Highcharts;
  chartGantt: Highcharts.Options = {
  xAxis: {
  min: Date.UTC(2023, 3, 1),
  max: Date.UTC(2023, 3, 31)
      },
  title: {
  text: 'IECE Inventory Controller Project Progress'
      },
  series: [{
  name: 'IECE Inventory Controller Project',
  type: 'gantt',
  data: [{
```

```
name: 'Start Project Requirement Analysis',
start: Date.UTC(2023, 3, 5),
end: Date.UTC(2023, 3, 15),
completed: 0.90
      },
      {
name: 'Development',
start: Date.UTC(2023, 3, 11),
end: Date.UTC(2023, 3, 22),
completed: {
amount: 0.35,
fill: 'green'
        }
      },
      {
name: 'Continuous Testing Software',
start: Date.UTC(2023, 3, 15),
end: Date.UTC(2023, 3, 29)
      }]
    }]
  };
}
```

In the xAxis section, you set the minimum (start date) and maximum date (end date) for the project.

In the series section, three new properties are added:

- start: This is the date-time property where you define the start date for the particular task.

- end: Here you set the end date-time for the specific task.

- completed: Here you can define how much in percentage a particular task is complete.

You define min and max, where the start date and end date are set; the completed property is required to fill the value of how much in percentage this particular part is complete.

Now copy Listing 6-32's code into `gantt-chart.component.html` to display the page.

Listing 6-32. gantt-chart.component.html

```
<div>
<highcharts-chart [Highcharts]="Highcharts" [constructorType]="'gan
ttChart'"
[options]="chartGantt" style="width: 100%; display: block;">
</highcharts-chart>
</div>
<router-outlet></router-outlet>
```

Once you run Listing 6-32's code, you will get the output shown in Figure 6-19.

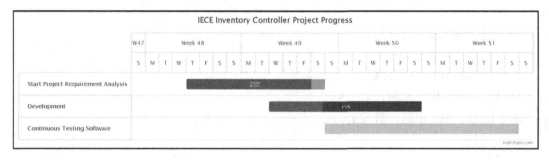

Figure 6-19. *Gantt chart demo with Highcharts*

More Charts

Deviation Chart

A deviation chart designed with two or more aligned bar charts. A graph displays a deviation relationship when it features how one or more sets of quantitative values differ from a reference set of values. Corporations and people from different fields uses deviation charts to gain better understanding of data.

For this demo, you are using a deviation chart as a step chart, where you will connect through steps. This chart is used for quality measures.

Formula:

max-min/no of steps = step size

Listing 6-33 shows the code to show the deviation chart. Here you are using a bell curve. Add this code to `deviation-chart.component.ts`.

Listing 6-33. deviation-chart.component.ts

```typescript
import { Component, OnInit } from '@angular/core';
import * as Highcharts from 'highcharts/highcharts';
import Bellcurve from 'highcharts/modules/histogram-bellcurve';
Bellcurve(Highcharts);
 @Component({
  selector: 'app-deviation-chart',
  templateUrl: './deviation-chart.component.html',
  styleUrls: ['./deviation-chart.component.css']
})
export class DeviationChartComponent {
  title = 'myHighChartsApp';
  Highcharts: typeof Highcharts = Highcharts;

  chartOptions: Highcharts.Options = {
  title: {
      text: 'Sample Count by Range'
    },
    xAxis: {
      min: 0,
      max: 4,
      tickInterval: 1
    },

    series: [{
      type: 'histogram',
      baseSeries: 's1',
      zIndex: -1,
      binsNumber: 5,
      color: 'transparent',
      borderWidth: 2,
      borderColor: 'green'
    }, {
```

```
        type: 'scatter',
        data: [0.17, 0.17, 0.18, 0.22, 0.26, 0.67, 0.98, 2.80,2.92, 3.30],
        id: 's1',
        visible: false,
        showInLegend: false
      }
    ]
    }
}
```

Run this app using ng serve and you will get the output shown in Figure 6-20. In the code, you have xAxis as minimum point 0 to max 4. The chart type is histogram. You connect this base series with s1 and its connect with the scatter data series. You make this chart visible and showInLegend as false.

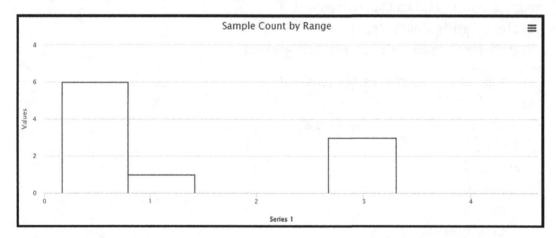

Figure 6-20. *Deviation chart*

Bubble Series Chart

A bubble chart is a comparative chart. It's an extension of scatter plots, which shows relationships of three values in the form of x,y,z; each dot relates to a single point.

Through a bubble chart you can get to know how many adults, kids, and old people are in different states of a country, so you can compare high or lower state populations in the country. When you require internal and external comparison you can choose this type of chart.

The upcoming example shows ABC Software sales in different countries in the form of market share, sales, and sales growth.

If you want to develop a Bubble chart, the following dependencies are required:

jQuery:

```
<script src="https://code.highcharts.com/highcharts.js"></script>
<script src="https://code.highcharts.com/highcharts-more.js"></script>
<script src="https://code.highcharts.com/modules/accessibility.
js"></script>
```

Angular:

```
import * as Highcharts from 'highcharts/highcharts';
import HighchartsMore from 'highcharts/highcharts-more';
HighchartsMore(Highcharts);
```

Listing 6-34 shows the code for the Bubble chart. Copy Listing 6-34's code into the bubble-chart.component.ts file.

Listing 6-34. bubble-chart.component.ts

```
import { Component, OnInit } from '@angular/core';
import * as Highcharts from 'highcharts/highcharts';
import HighchartsMore from 'highcharts/highcharts-more';
HighchartsMore(Highcharts);
interface ExtendedPointOptionsObject extends Highcharts.
PointOptionsObject {
  country: string;
}
@Component({
  selector: 'app-bubble-chart',
  templateUrl: './bubble-chart.component.html',
  styleUrls: ['./bubble-chart.component.css']
})
export class BubbleChartComponent {
  title = 'myHighChartsApp';
  Highcharts: typeof Highcharts = Highcharts;
  chartOptions: Highcharts.Options = {
```

```
chart: {
  type: 'bubble',
  plotBorderWidth: 1,
},
legend: {
  enabled: false,
},
title: {
  text: 'Total Revenue for ABC Software (Country wise)',
},
xAxis: {
  gridLineWidth: 1,
  title: {
    text: 'Market Share',
  },
  labels: {
    format: '{value} ',
  },
},
yAxis: {
    startOnTick: false,
    endOnTick: false,
    title: {
      text: 'Sales in CR',
    },
    labels: {
      format: '{value} $',
    },
    maxPadding: 0.2,
  },
tooltip: {
    useHTML: true,
    headerFormat: '<table>',
    pointFormat:
      '<tr><th colspan="2"><h3>{point.country}</h3></th></tr>' +
```

```
        '<tr><th>Market Share:</th><td>{point.x} %</td></tr>' +
        '<tr><th>Sales:</th><td>{point.y} Cr</td></tr>' +
        '<tr><th>Sales Growth:</th><td>{point.z}%</td></tr>',
      footerFormat: '</table>',
      followPointer: true,
    },
    plotOptions: {
      series: {
        dataLabels: {
          enabled: true,
          format: '{point.name}',
        },
      },
    },
    series: [
      {
        type: 'bubble',
        data: [
          { x: 40, y: 70, z: 80, name: 'DE', country: 'Germany' },
          { x: 45, y: 70, z: 135, name: 'FI', country: 'Finland' },
          { x: 35, y: 68, z: 180, name: 'ES', country: 'Spain' },
          { x: 30, y: 45, z: 142, name: 'FR', country: 'France' },
          { x: 55, y: 65, z: 190, name: 'IN', country: 'India' },
        ] as Array<ExtendedPointOptionsObject>,
      },
    ],
  };
}
```

In the series section you have x, y, z, name, and country, where x denotes market share, y denotes sales, z denotes sales growth, and the name section denotes country code.

Next, the chart type is bubble because here you construct a bubble series.

In the plotOptions: you can define dataLabels so here you set point format for name.

```
plotOptions: {
  series: {
    dataLabels: {
      enabled: true,
      format: '{point.name}',
    },
  },
},
```

If you run the above code, your bubble series will look like Figure 6-21.

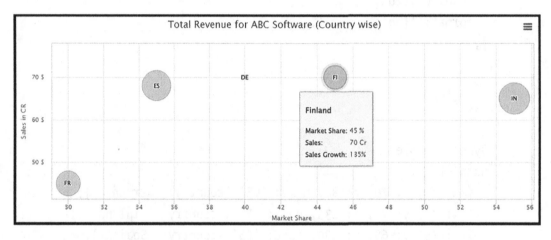

Figure 6-21. *Bubble series chart*

Custom Tooltip in Highcharts

Listing 6-34 shows a custom format for a tooltip so you can set your tooltip and show information in your way. You can add HTML tags and CSS design also. For a bubble chart, you must show values in the form of x, y, and z. See the following code:

```
tooltip: {
    useHTML: true,
    headerFormat: '<table>',
    pointFormat:
    '<tr><thcolspan="2"><h3>{point.country}</h3></th></tr>' +
      '<tr><th>Market Share:</th><td>{point.x} %</td></tr>' +
      '<tr><th>Sales:</th><td>{point.y} Cr</td></tr>' +
```

```
      '<tr><th>Sales Growth:</th><td>{point.z}%</td></tr>',
    footerFormat: '</table>',
    followPointer: true,
  },
```

Here you set useHTML: true, headerformat, pointFormat, footerFormat, and followPointer.

Dependency Wheel

A dependency wheel chart is an attractive connecting node chart that is useful to visualize relations between two dependent nodes (elements) in the chart. Its nodes are connected and drawn within a circle.

In Listing 6-35, you will see how many employees are shifting their job from one company to another. They are encoded by connector width to visualize employee shifting volume and color to illustrate the company, slightly desaturated for better visibility. Copy the code into dependency-wheel-chart.ts.

Listing 6-35. dependency-wheel-chart.component.ts

```
import { Component, OnInit } from '@angular/core';
import * as Highcharts from 'highcharts/highcharts';
import sankey from 'highcharts/modules/sankey';
import dependencywheel from 'highcharts/modules/dependency-wheel';
import accesibility from 'highcharts/modules/accessibility';
sankey(Highcharts);
dependencywheel(Highcharts);
accesibility(Highcharts);
@Component({
  selector: 'app-dependency-wheel-chart',
templateUrl: './dependency-wheel-chart.component.html',
styleUrls: ['./dependency-wheel-chart.component.css']
})
export class DependencyWheelChartComponent {
  title = 'myHighChartsApp';
  Highcharts: typeof Highcharts = Highcharts;
chartOptions: Highcharts.Options = {
```

```
    accessibility: {
      point: {
valueDescriptionFormat: '{index}. From {point.from} to {point.to}: {point.
weight}.'
      }
    },
title:{
      text: 'Employees Shifting from one Company to another ',
    },
    series: [{
      keys: ['from', 'to', 'weight'],
      data: [
        ['ABCCorp', 'WinCorp', 7],
        ['ABCCorp', 'FinTech', 3],
        ['ABCCorp', 'RoseInc', 3],
        ['ABCCorp', 'GIL', 2],
        ['GIL', 'RoseInc', 8],
        ['GIL', 'WinCorp', 7],
        ['GIL', 'MaxInc', 3],
        ['MaxInc', 'JbnInc', 2],
        ['MaxInc', 'JIL', 8],
        ['MaxInc', 'GIL', 4],
        ['MaxInc', 'RoseInc', 2],
        ['USCorp', 'PSInc', 4],
        ['USCorp', 'JIL', 1],
        ['USCorp', 'JbnInc', 1],
        ['USCorp', 'WinCorp', 5],
        ['JbnCorp', 'JIL', 2],
        ['JbnCorp', 'PsInc', 1],
        ['PsInc', 'JILInc', 3],
        ['PsInc', 'JbnInc', 3],
        ['KenFinTech', 'NPS', 2],
        ['KenFinTech', 'JLL', 5],
        ['NPS', 'USCorp', 3],
        ['JLL', 'RoseInc', 3],
```

```
        ['RoseInc', 'UsCorp', 2],
        ['EksInfotech', 'RoseInc', 8],
        ['PsInc', 'JVC', 7],
        ['JBCInc', 'CCDCorp', 9],
        ['BCCI', 'JLL', 10],
        ['WIL', 'MFR', 3],
      ],
      type: 'dependencywheel',
      name: 'Dependency wheel series',
dataLabels: {
        color: '#333',
        style: {
textOutline: 'none'
        },
textPath: {
          enabled: true
        },
        distance: 10
      },
      size: '95%'
    }]
}
}
```

Here you have chart type of dependencywheel. In the series section, you have keys of from, to, and weight. In the form section, you have where an employee was working previously. There is a section for a new company, and weight denotes the number of employees moving from one company to another.

The data property is array-based property where you can build your collection based on your keys.

If you run this code, it looks like Figure 6-22.

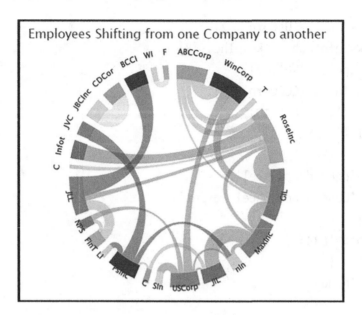

Figure 6-22. Dependency wheel chart

Error Bar Series

Error bar charts are used to understand uncertainty or error in data. You can apply an error chart in a scatter chart. Error bar charts to provide additional layers for detail about the uncertainty. With the error bar chart you can find out standard deviation and confidence interval very easily.

This example shows how a company completes an order and how far they are from the completion. Months are on the x-Axis and two y-Axes denote work orders and order completion.

If you want to create an error bar chart using Highcharts, the following dependencies are required:

jQuery:

```
<script src="https://code.highcharts.com/highcharts.js"></script>
<script src="https://code.highcharts.com/highcharts-more.js"></script>
<script src="https://code.highcharts.com/modules/accessibility.js"></script>
```

Angular:

```
import * as Highcharts from 'highcharts/highcharts';
import HighChartsMore from 'highcharts/highcharts-more';
import Accessability from 'highcharts/modules/accessibility';
HighChartsMore(Highcharts);
Accessability(Highcharts);
```

Now copy the code in Listing 6-36 into error-bar-chart.ts.

Listing 6-36. error-bar-chart.component.ts

```
import { Component, OnInit } from '@angular/core';
import * as Highcharts from 'highcharts/highcharts';
import HighChartsMore from 'highcharts/highcharts-more';
import Accessability from 'highcharts/modules/accessibility';
HighChartsMore(Highcharts);
Accessability(Highcharts);
interface ExtendedChartOptions extends Highcharts.ChartOptions {
zoomType: string;
}
@Component({
  selector: 'app-error-bar-chart',
templateUrl: './error-bar-chart.component.html',
styleUrls: ['./error-bar-chart.component.css']
})
export class ErrorBarChartComponent {
  title = 'myHighChartsApp';
  Highcharts: typeof Highcharts = Highcharts;
chartOptions: Highcharts.Options = {
    chart: {
zoomType: 'xy'
    } as ExtendedChartOptions,
    title: {
      text: 'Orders vs Completion'
    },
xAxis: [{
```

```
        categories: ['Jan', 'Feb', 'Mar', 'Apr', 'May', 'Jun', 'Jul', 'Aug',
        'Sep', 'Oct', 'Nov', 'Dec']
    }],
yAxis: [{ // Primary yAxis
        labels: {
          format: '{value} $',
          style: {
            color: 'DarkOliveGreen',
          }
        },
        title: {
          text: 'WorkOrders',
          style: {
            color: 'DarkOliveGreen',
          }
        }
    }, { // Secondary yAxis
        title: {
          text: 'Complition',
          style: {
            color: 'DarkRed'
          }
        },
        labels: {
          format: '{value} %',
          style: {
            color: 'DarkRed'
          }
        },
        opposite: true
    }],
    tooltip: {
      shared: true
    },
    series: [{
```

```
        name: 'Complition',
        type: 'column',
yAxis: 1,
        data: [49.9, 71.5, 99.4, 88.2, 100.0, 99.0, 67.6, 48.5, 26.4, 94.1,
        97.6, 54.4],
        tooltip: {
pointFormat: '<span style="font-weight: bold; color: {series.
color}">{series.name}</span>: <b>{point.y:.1f} </b> '
        }
    }, {
        name: 'Complition error',
        type: 'errorbar',
yAxis: 1,
        data: [[43, 52], [62, 69], [91, 99], [82, 100], [40, 50], [71, 79],
        [35, 43], [42, 49], [20, 22], [89, 99], [91, 98], [52, 56]],
        tooltip: {
pointFormat: '(error range: {point.low}-{point.high} )<br/>'
        }
    }, {
        name: 'WorkOrders',
        type: 'spline',
        data: [7.1, 6.7, 8.5, 12.5, 16.2, 19.5, 22.2, 24.5, 22.3, 17.3,
        11.9, 9.2],
        tooltip: {
pointFormat: '<span style="font-weight: bold; color: {series.
color}">{series.name}</span>: <b>{point.y:.1f}</b> '
        }
    }, {
        name: 'WorkOrder error',
        type: 'errorbar',
        data: [[5, 8], [5.3, 7.4], [8.6, 10.2], [14.1, 15.2], [16, 19.1],
        [20.0, 22.0], [21.2, 24.3], [26.3, 27.7], [23.1, 23.7], [17.0,
        19.1], [10.9, 13.0], [7.2, 9.0]],
        tooltip: {
pointFormat: '(error range: {point.low}-{point.high})<br/>'
```

```
        }
    }],
  }
}
```

In the series section are chart types of `errorbar` and `spline` to find out the difference between orders and completion. If you run this code, you will get the output shown in Figure 6-23.

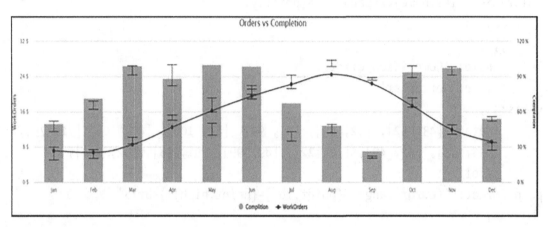

Figure 6-23. *Error bar chart*

Lollipop Chart

The lollipop chart is the same as a bar chart, but visually it looks differently. It consists of a line and a dot at the end. Lollipop charts are used to compare larger values. The center of the circle of the lollipop denotes the values.

If you want to draw a lollipop chart using Highcharts, the following dependencies are required:

jQuery:

```
<script src="https://code.highcharts.com/highcharts.js"></script>
<script src="https://code.highcharts.com/highcharts-more.js"></script>
<script src="https://code.highcharts.com/modules/dumbbell.js"></script>
<script src="https://code.highcharts.com/modules/lollipop.js"></script>
```

Angular:

```
import * as Highcharts from "highcharts";
import More from "highcharts/highcharts-more";
import Dumbell from "highcharts/modules/dumbbell";
import Lollipop from "highcharts/modules/lollipop";
```

Copy the code in Listing 6-37 into `lolipop-chart.component.ts`.

Listing 6-37. lolipop-chart.component.ts

```
import { Component, OnInit } from '@angular/core';
import * as Highcharts from "highcharts";
import More from "highcharts/highcharts-more";
import Dumbell from "highcharts/modules/dumbbell";
import Lollipop from "highcharts/modules/lollipop";
More(Highcharts);
Dumbell(Highcharts);
Lollipop(Highcharts);
@Component({
  selector: 'app-lolipop-chart',
templateUrl: './lolipop-chart.component.html',
styleUrls: ['./lolipop-chart.component.css']
})
export class LolipopChartComponent {
  Highcharts: typeof Highcharts = Highcharts;
chartOptions: Highcharts.Options = {
    accessibility: {
      point: {
valueDescriptionFormat: '{index}. {xDescription}, {point.y}.'
      }
    },
    legend: {
      enabled: false
    },
    subtitle: {
      text: '2022'
    },
```

```
      title: {
        text: 'BRICS Countries Population'
      },
      tooltip: {
        shared: true
      },
xAxis: {
        type: 'category'
      },
yAxis: {
        title: {
          text: 'Population'
        }
      },
      series: [{
        type: 'lollipop',
        name: 'Population',
        data: [{
          name: 'Brazil',
          low: 216082487 ,
        }, {
          name: 'Russia',
          low: 146080304
        }, {
          name: 'India',
          low: 1417173173
        }, {
          name: 'China',
          low: 1425887337
        }, {
          name: 'South Africa',
          low: 59893885
        }]
      }]
  };
}
```

Here you use dumbbell and lollipop dependencies. In the series section the chart type is lollipop and you require a data array. In the name section are countries and in the low properties are population counts. If you run this code, you will get the output shown in Figure 6-24.

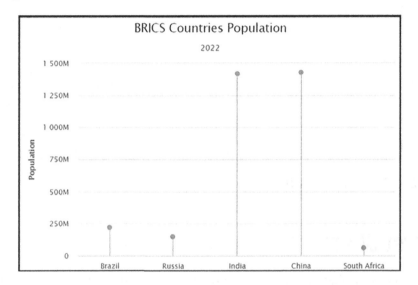

Figure 6-24. *Lollipop chart*

If you want to change this chart to vertical, you can set the `inverted` property as `true`.

```
chart: {
inverted : true,
    },
```

If you run this code, you will get the output shown in Figure 6-25.

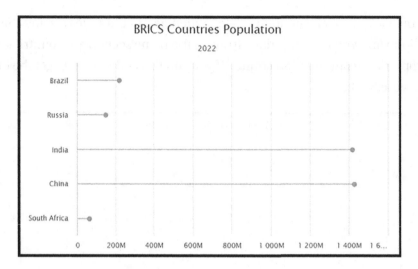

Figure 6-25. *Vertical lollipop chart*

Sunburst Chart

A sunburst chart is designed to display hierarchical data structures where the hierarchy is represented by a circle. The center represents the root node of the tree. Each circle defines a different hierarchy. In a sunburst chart, you can easily define a layered data structure. For example, say you want to represent a factory plant production globally. In each layer you can easily define country data, state data, and city data.

To generate a sunburst chart, the following dependencies are required:

jQuery:

```
<script src="https://code.highcharts.com/highcharts.js"></script>
<script src="https://code.highcharts.com/modules/sunburst.js"></script>
```

Angular:

```
import * as Highcharts from "highcharts";
import HC_sunburst from "highcharts/modules/sunburst";
HC_sunburst(Highcharts);
```

This example shows IECE Digital Employees strength worldwide, so copy the code in Listing 6-38 into `sunburst-chart.component.ts`.

Listing 6-38. sunburst-chart.component.ts

```typescript
import { Component, OnInit } from '@angular/core';
import * as Highcharts from "highcharts";
import HC_sunburst from "highcharts/modules/sunburst";
HC_sunburst(Highcharts);
@Component({
  selector: 'app-sunburst-chart',
templateUrl: './sunburst-chart.component.html',
styleUrls: ['./sunburst-chart.component.css']
})
export class SunburstChartComponent {
  title = 'myHighChartsApp';
  Highcharts: typeof Highcharts = Highcharts;
chartOptions: Highcharts.Options = {
    // Let the center circle be transparent
    colors: ['green'],
    title: {
      text: "IECE Digital Employees strength worldwide"
    },
    series: [
      {
        type: "sunburst",
        data: [
          {
            id: "0.0",
            parent: "",
            name: "IECE Group"
          },
          {
            id: "1.1",
            parent: "0.0",
            name: "Asia",
            value: 100000
          },
          {
```

```
      id: "2.1",
      parent: "1.1",
      name: "India",
      value: 50000
    },
    {
     id: "3.1",
      parent: "2.1",
      name: "Delhi",
      value: 10000
    },
    {
      id: "3.2",
      parent: "2.1",
      name: "Bangalore",
      value: 30000
    },
    {
      id: "3.3",
      parent: "2.1",
      name: "Chennai",
      value: 10000
    },
    {
      id: "2.2",
      parent: "1.1",
      name: "Japan",
      value: 20000
    },
    {
      id: "3.4",
      parent: "2.2",
      name: "Tokyo",
      value: 20000
    },
```

```
  {
    id: "2.3",
    parent: "1.1",
    name: "Philippines",
    value: 30000
  },
  {
    id: "3.5",
    parent: "2.3",
    name: "Manila",
    value: 30000
  },
  {
    id: "1.2",
    parent: "0.0",
    name: "America",
    value: 50000
  },
  {
    id: "2.4",
    parent: "1.2",
    name: "North America",
    value: 25000
  },
  {
    id: "3.6",
    parent: "2.4",
    name: "New York",
    value: 10000
  },
  {
    id: "3.6",
    parent: "2.4",
    name: "Montreal",
    value: 10000
```

```
        },
        {
          id: "3.6",
          parent: "2.4",
          name: "Mexico",
          value: 5000
        },
        {
          id: "2.5",
          parent: "1.2",
          name: "South America",
          value: 25000
        },
        {
          id: "3.8",
          parent: "2.5",
          name: "Rosario",
          value: 25000
        },
      ],
      name: "Root",
allowTraversingTree: true,
levelIsConstant: false,
      cursor: "pointer",
dataLabels: {
        format: "{point.name}",
        filter: {
          property: "innerArcLength",
          operator: ">",
          value: 16
        },
rotationMode: "circular"
      },
      levels: [
        {
```

```
            level: 1,
dataLabels: {
                filter: {
                  property: "outerArcLength",
                  operator: ">",
                  value: 64
                }
            },
          },
          {
            level: 2,
            color:'darkgreen'
          },
          {
            level: 3,
colorVariation: {
                key: "brightness",
                to: -0.5
              },
            color:'lightblue'
          },
          {
            level: 4,
colorVariation: {
                key: "brightness",
                to: 0.5,

              },
            color:'darkred'
          }
      ]
      }
    ],
    tooltip: {
headerFormat: "",
pointFormat:
```

```
        "Total Employees of <b>{point.name}</b> is <b>{point.value}</b>"
    }
  };
}
```

Here the chart type is sunburst. The layer data array is very important; it's built with id, parent, and name. For the main layer, the id is 0.0 and the parent is string.empty. For the next subsequent layer, the id is 1.1 and the parent is 0.0; this is how you connect layer 0 to layer 1.

Layer 0 is for company name, Layer 1 is for continent, Layer 2 is for countries, and Layer 3 is for cities.

Notice allowTraversingTree: true. This property is designed for traversing features in sunburst charts. The benefit of this property is that when a user clicks on any layer, its related layer will be round.

In the levels array, you can define each layer property and set here data labels, colors, and brightness.

If you run the code in Listing 6-38, you will get the output shown in Figure 6-26.

Figure 6-26. *Sunburst chart*

If you click on Layer 1 or Layer 2, you will get subsequent details. See Figure 6-27.

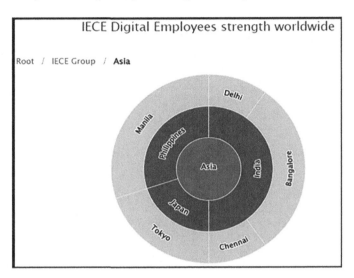

Figure 6-27. *Sunburst chart with allowTraversingTree: true*

If `allowTraversingTree: true`, then if you click on any layer, you will get subsequent layers in detail. In Figure 6-27, you get the Layer links as well from the root level to the current main layer.

Summary

In this chapter, you saw how easily you can set themes and styles and make your charts more interactive and understandable. You also saw additional charts like 3D charts, organizational charts, Gantt charts, timelines, deviation charts, and sunburst charts plus dependency wheels and bell curves. Highcharts is a stunning tool, and you can develop any chart based on your requirements. In the next chapter, I will go over how to build a real-time dashboard using Highcharts.

CHAPTER 7

Building a Real-Time Dashboard

Sourabh Mishra[a*]

 [a] IECE Digital, Bangalore, India

In this chapter, you will learn how to show multiple real-time charts in a dashboard. To understand better how to easily consume a web API and develop a real-time dashboard, you will create one sample learning application. In this chapter, you will also learn some advanced concepts of Angular routing and the Forms module in order to quickly build your interactive app with the use of Angular and Highcharts.

Real-Time Dashboard Application

In this sample learning e-portfolio application, you are going to develop features that provide live historical data from the stock market. Users can generate a portfolio of any stock and check their profit/loss. They can also check top loser and gainer stocks so that they can make better decisions about their investments. The idea behind developing this app is so you can understand and learn how easy it is to design interactive apps with the use of Angular and Highcharts. The app will have two sections:

- Market radar section
- Dashboard section

© Sourabh Mishra 2023
S. Mishra, *Practical Highcharts with Angular*, https://doi.org/10.1007/978-1-4842-9181-8_7

For the market radar, the user can add their favorite stock into a database. Then they can select stock names, dates, and periods such as a daily or monthly basis, and they can see the performance of a particular stock very quickly.

In the dashboard section, users can analyze how much they invested and whether they have a profit or loss.

In Chapter 5, I talked about how you can easily consume a web API with Angular using .NET Core. For this application, you'll use the same Angular project, and if you want, you can develop a new Angular application using the Angular CLI, which I discussed in Chapter 3.

This app is designed with a client-server architecture model where you have two different projects. One is the UI side, which you develop in Angular with Highcharts. For the server side, you'll develop a .NET 6-based web API.

Features of the App

For this app, the user will get two menus:

- **Market Radar**: The user can select whatever stocks you inserted into the database from a drop-down list, with parameters of From Date, End Date, and a period type in the form of daily and monthly. Once the user clicks the Search button, the basis of the selected conditions will generate a chart.

- **Dashboard**: In this section, the user can check their list of invested stocks. They can see a profit/loss portfolio chart and a top gainer/loser investment chart. This app will give them a better idea about their investments using Highcharts.

Creating a Web API

For this application, you'll create a web API with the use of Visual Studio. Go to File ➤ New Project ➤ Select ➤ ASP.NET Core Web API Application (.NET 6) (Figure 7-1). In Chapter 5, you saw how to develop a web API using .NET 6. See Figure 7-1.

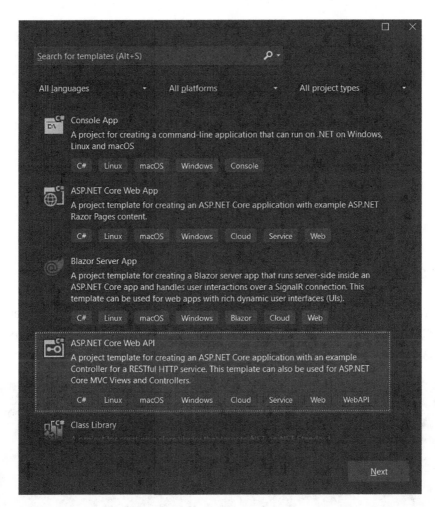

Figure 7-1. *Creating a new project*

Click the Next button (Figure 7-2).

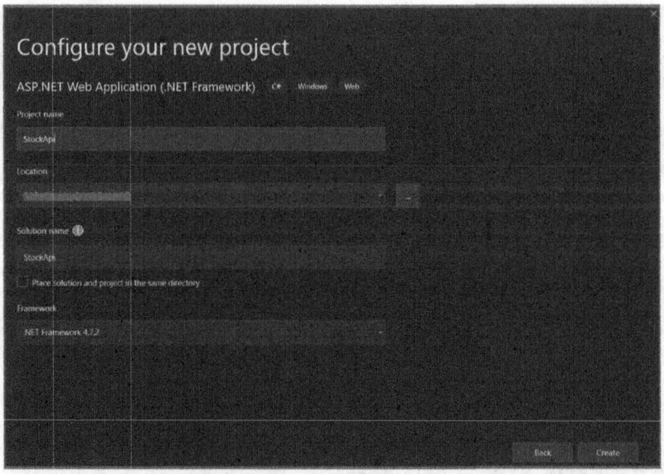

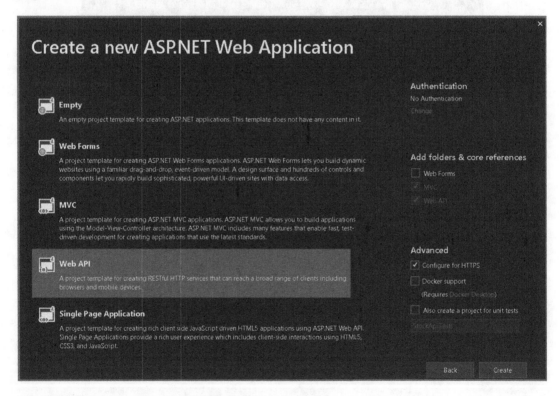

Figure 7-2. *Configuring a new project*

Here, you must provide the project name and you can choose the .NET 6 version. Click the Create button to go to the Create a new ASP.NET Web Application screen (Figure 7-3).

Figure 7-3. *Creating a new web API application*

Click the Next button. You can see that your web API creation has completed. In the first step, you will call CORS-related dependencies because this web API will be consumed by the Angular app. Open Solution Explorer and right-click into the project and choose the Manage NuGet Package option (Figure 7-4).

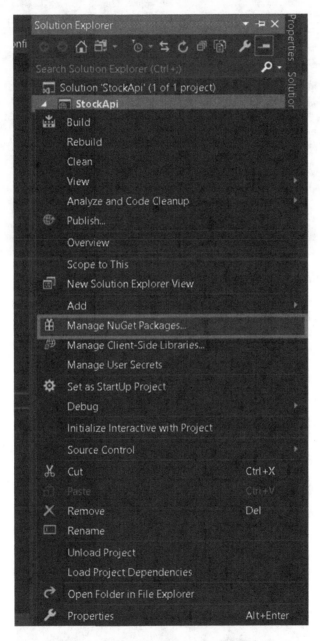

***Figure 7-4.** Managing the NuGet package for the project*

Search for Microsoft.AspNet.WebApi.Cors. You will get the same list, so choose
Microsoft.AspNet.WebApi.Cors and click the Install button (Figure 7-5).

Figure 7-5. *Installing Microsoft.AspNet.WebApi.Cors*

Now click the OK button (Figure 7-6).

Figure 7-6. *Installing the NugetPacakge for the project*

Click the I Accept button. After this step, the NuGet package installation will complete.

Now it's time to set CORS, so open Solution Explorer ➤ Open Program.cs and copy Listing 7-1's code.

Listing 7-1. Program.cs

```
var builder = WebApplication.CreateBuilder(args);
// Add services to the container.
builder.Services.AddCors(options =>
{
    options.AddDefaultPolicy(
        builder =>
        {
            builder.WithOrigins("http://localhost:4200")
                            .AllowAnyHeader()
                            .AllowAnyMethod();
        });
});

builder.Services.AddControllers();
// Learn more about configuring Swagger/OpenAPI at https://aka.ms/
aspnetcore/swashbuckle
builder.Services.AddEndpointsApiExplorer();
builder.Services.AddSwaggerGen();

var app = builder.Build();

app.UseCors(builder =>
{
    builder
    .AllowAnyOrigin()
    .AllowAnyMethod()
    .AllowAnyHeader();
});
```

```
// Configure the HTTP request pipeline.
if (app.Environment.IsDevelopment())
{
    app.UseSwagger();
    app.UseSwaggerUI();
}

app.UseAuthorization();

app.MapControllers();

app.Run();
```

In this code, you enable CORS and CORS attributes so you can send a request from the Angular application to the web API very quickly. Here you add DefaultPolicy for CORS where you set the origin's URL, headers, and methods.

For related learning about CORS, please refer to Chapter 5 where I describe CORS in more detail.

Setting Up a Database

This learning application requires one database because you want to work with live data. In this section, you are going to develop a database called StockDb. StockDb contains one table called StockMaster where you store your stock-related information. For real-time information, you will get data from a NuGet service, which is the Alpha Vantage API.

Let's create the database. Here you'll use Visual Studio, but you can also choose the platform per your requirements.

To create a database in Visual Studio, go to View ➤ SQL Server Object Explorer. Open a connection and right-click into the Database folder and select Add New Database (Figure 7-7).

Figure 7-7. *Adding a new database using Visual Studio*

Once you click Add New Database, you will get the screen shown in Figure 7-8. Set the database name and click the OK button.

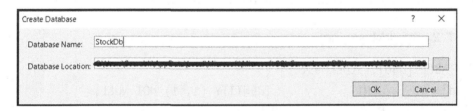

Figure 7-8. *Create Database screen*

Your database has been created. Now it's time to create the table. Expand `StockDb` and right-click the `Table` folder and choose Add New Table (Figure 7-9).

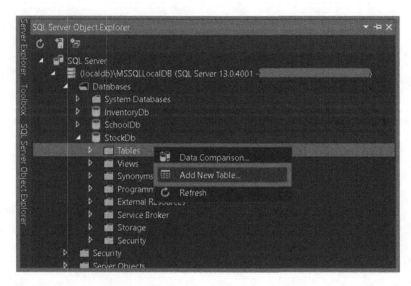

Figure 7-9. *Add New Table screen*

Now add the script in Listing 7-2 into the T-Sql Section (Figure 7-10).

Listing 7-2. StockMaster.sql

```
CREATE TABLE [dbo].[StockMaster] (
    [Id]        INT             IDENTITY (1, 1) NOT NULL,
    [StockId]   NVARCHAR (50) NULL,
    [StockName] NVARCHAR (50) NULL,
    [BuyPrice]  DECIMAL (18)  NULL,
    [Qty]       DECIMAL (18)  NULL,
    [IsActive]  BIT             NULL,
    PRIMARY KEY CLUSTERED ([Id] ASC)
);
```

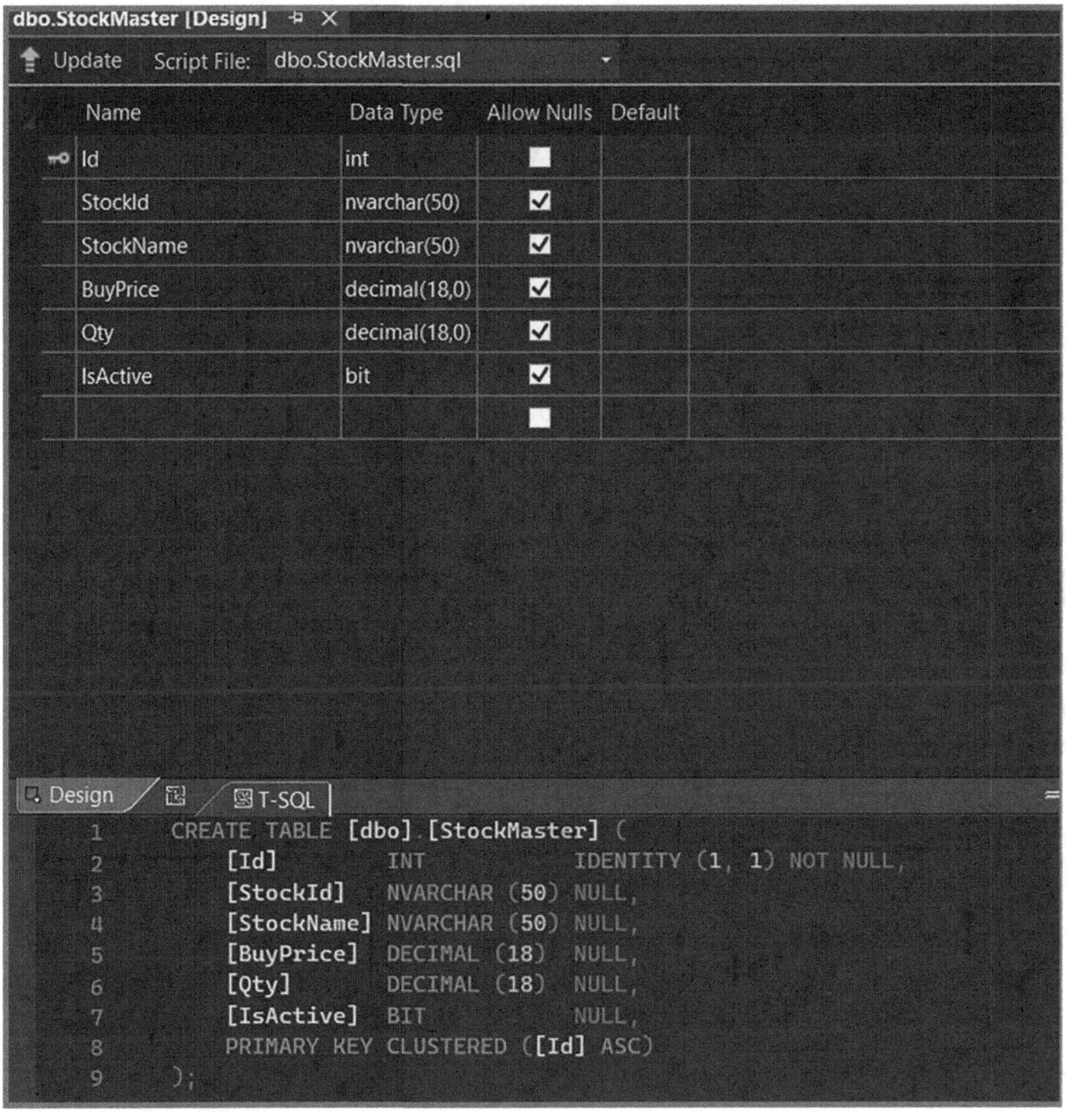

Figure 7-10. *Adding the table script*

Click the Update button. After that, you will get one dialog box so choose Update Database and your table will be updated. Right-click into the StockMaster table and select ViewData. Now you can enter some data (Figure 7-11). While entering data remember you have to add the proper stockId, so if you go to the NASDAQ website you will get correct the stockId for each stock. For example, Microsoft is MSFT, Arcelormittale is MT, Google is GOOGL, and Infosys is infy. Please find your correct stockIds and fill in the database table.

249

Id	StockId	StockName	BuyPrice	Qty	IsActive
1	MSFT	Microsoft	50	10	True
2	ibm	IBM	105	5	True
3	abb	ABB	NULL	NULL	False
4	GOOGL	google	NULL	NULL	False
5	MT	Arcelor Mittal	NULL	NULL	False
6	infy	Infosys	150	20	True
NULL	NULL	NULL	NULL	NULL	NULL

Figure 7-11. *Adding data manually into a table*

Creating a Database-First Approach Using Entity Framework Core

In this section, you will set up a database-first approach with Entity Framework Core. For more detail about the database-first approach and Entity Framework, refer to Chapter 5, where I talk in detail about this process.

For the database-first approach in Entity Framework Core, you need some dependencies from NuGet. Follow these steps.

Step 1: Go to the Package Manager Console and type these commands one by one:

```
Install-Package Microsoft.Entityframeworkcore.SqlServer
```

```
Install-Package Microsoft.Entityframeworkcore.design
```

```
Install-Package Microsoft.Entityframeworkcore.tools
```

Step 2. Create a folder called Models.

Step 3. Now it's time to scaffold the db. With this method you can set provider, connection string, and output directory name, so copy and paste following command and do the necessary changes:

```
scaffold-dbcontext -provider Microsoft.Entityframeworkcore.sqlserver
-connection "Data Source=(localdb)\MSSQLLocalDB; Initial Catalog=StockDb"
-OutputDir Models
```

The first command is `scaffold-dbcontext`. Here you have to provide `EntitiyFrameworkcore.Sqlserver`, the established connection data source which you can take from your data source (this part you have to change based on your local setting). In the next part, you have to set your database name, which is `StockDb`, and then last but not the least is the output directory, which you have set as `Models`.

If you open the `Models` folder, you will get two files: the first is `StockdbContext` and the second is `StockMaster`.

`StockDbContext` is the main file that denotes the db structure; this instance will be required in the db operations. `StockMaster` is the table you created in the db.

Now the database-first settings using Entity Framework Core are completed. The next step is to set up the NASDAQ API.

In this application, for learning purposes, you will use the Alpha Vantage Finance API so people can get real-time data from the stock market.

For this process, you require the following dependencies:

Step 1. Install the first dependency from the NuGet Package Manger console.

```
Install-Package AlphaVantage.Net.Core -Version 2.0.1
```

This one is the basic dependency for the Alpha Vantage API for .NET core.

Step 2. Install one more dependency, which is

```
Install-Package AlphaVantage.Net.Stocks -Version 2.0.1
```

This one is required to install the stock API.

Now add new folder called `ProjectModels` and add a `Model` class. This will help in future development, so for this application you'll create a `StockModel` class. For this, go to Solution Explorer and right-Click in the `Model` class and provide the name for the class and click the Add button. Now add Listing 7-3's code to this `StockModel` class.

Listing 7-3. StockModel.cs

```
using System;
using System.Collections.Generic;
using System.Linq;
using System.Web;

namespace Alpha.Models
{
    public class StockModel
```

```
    {
        public string StockId { get; set; }
        public string StockName { get; set; }
        public string Date { get; set; }
        public decimal Open { get; set; }
        public decimal High { get; set; }
        public decimal Low { get; set; }
        public decimal Close { get; set; }
        public decimal Volume { get; set; }
        public decimal? BuyPrice { get; set; }
        public decimal? Qty { get; set; }
        public bool IsActive { get; set; }
        public decimal? TotalInvested { get; set; }
        public decimal? CurrentValue { get; set; }
        public decimal? TotalGain { get; set; }
    }
}
```

Now it's time to create an API controller where you can write your business logic. Open Solution Explorer, right-click in the Controller folder and Add ➤ Controller ➤ Select Web API 2 Controller – Empty from the list (Figure 7-12).

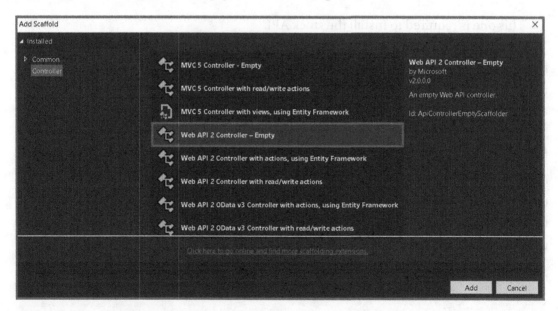

Figure 7-12. *Adding a new web API controller*

Click the Add button. You will get the Add Controller screen. Provide your controller name. For this application, use StockController. After this action, you will see the StockController added into your `Controller` folder. This controller will start to add some methods, which will help to fetch and insert data.

Let's understand the methods.

- `AddStock()`: This method is used to add the new stock into the `StockMaster` table. In this method, you require a `StockId`. In this particular field, you have to provide a stock short name; every company has an alias in NASDAQ. For example, Microsoft is MSFT, Infosys is INFY, and Google is GOOGL. You can quickly get these names from the NASDAQ website (for help, you can refer to Figure 7-11). The Alpha Vantage Finance API will track data based on this stock id only, so please carefully add the stock ids; otherwise, data will not come. Then you need the stock name, buy price, total stock quantity, and `IsActive`. You write this method with the use of the Entity Framework.

- `GetStock()`: This method will fetch all active records from the `StockMaster` table and display the stock collection in the dropdown list for the market radar screen.

- `GetStockData()`: With the use of this method, the user can search their stock performance based on stock id, start date, end date, and period. This method helps explore stock performance based on time.

- `GetActiveStock()`: This method provides the list of stocks where `IsActive = true` in the `StockMaster` table.

- `GetDashboardPortfolioData()`: This method provides a list of active stocks, total investment, current value of shares, and total gain so you can predict and develop charts very quickly.

- `GetGainerLoserStockData()`: This method provides data for the top gainer and top loser stock from the `StockMaster` table.

- `GetStockClosingPrice()`: This method is used for getting stock information using the Alpha Vantage API. It requires `stockId` and interval type information into `GetTimeSeriesAsync` method.

Now copy Listing 7-4's code into the StockController.cs file.

Listing 7-4. StockController.cs

```
using Microsoft.AspNetCore.Http;
using Microsoft.AspNetCore.Mvc;
using AlphaVantage.Net.Core.Client;
using AlphaVantage.Net.Stocks;
using AlphaVantage.Net.Stocks.Client;
using AlphaVantage.Net.Common.Size;
using AlphaVantage.Net.Common.Intervals;
using Microsoft.AspNetCore.Cors;
using NodaTime;
using Interval = AlphaVantage.Net.Common.Intervals.Interval;
using Microsoft.IdentityModel.Tokens;
using StockApi.Models;
using StockApi.ProjectModels;

namespace StockApi.Controllers
{
    [EnableCors()] // this is required to enable cors
    [Route("api/[controller]")]
    [ApiController]
    public class StockController : ControllerBase
    {
        StockDbContext stockDbEntities = null;
        List<StockModel> stockModels = new List<StockModel>();

        private async Task<object> GetStockClosingPrice(string stockId,
        DateTime startDate, DateTime endDate)
        {
            string apiKey = "2";
            using var client = new AlphaVantageClient(apiKey);
            using var stocksClient = client.Stocks();

            StockTimeSeries stockTs = await stocksClient.
            GetTimeSeriesAsync(stockId, Interval.Daily, OutputSize.
            Compact, isAdjusted: true);
```

```
    var query = stockTs.DataPoints.Where(c => c.Time >= startDate
    && c.Time <= endDate);
    return query.LastOrDefault().ClosingPrice;
}

[Route("~/api/GetDashboardPortfolioData")]
[HttpGet]
public List<StockModel> GetDashboardPortfolioData()
{
    var startDate = DateTime.UtcNow.AddDays(-5);
    var endDate = DateTime.UtcNow;
    stockDbEntities = new StockDbContext();
    var stockmasters = stockDbEntities.StockMasters
    .Where(x => x.IsActive == true).ToList();

    stockmasters.ForEach(x =>
    {
        var stockClosingData = GetStockClosingPrice(x.StockId,
        startDate, endDate).Result;
        if (stockClosingData != null)
        {
            StockModel stockModel = new StockModel();
            stockModel.StockId = x.StockId;
            stockModel.StockName = x.StockName;
            stockModel.BuyPrice = x.BuyPrice;
            stockModel.Qty = x.Qty;
            stockModel.TotalInvested = x.Qty * x.BuyPrice;
            stockModel.CurrentValue = x.Qty * (decimal)
            stockClosingData;
            stockModel.TotalGain = stockModel.CurrentValue -
            stockModel.TotalInvested;
            stockModels.Add(stockModel);
        }
    });
    return stockModels.OrderBy(c => c.TotalGain).ToList();
}
```

```
[Route("~/api/GetStock")]
[HttpGet]
public List<StockModel> GetStock()
{
    stockDbEntities = new StockDbContext();
    List<StockModel> stockModels = new List<StockModel>();
    var query = stockDbEntities.StockMasters.ToList();
    query.ForEach(x =>
    {
        StockModel stockModel = new StockModel();
        stockModel.StockId = x.StockId;
        stockModel.StockName = x.StockName;
        stockModels.Add(stockModel);
    });
    return stockModels;
}
[Route("~/api/AlphaAdvantage/AddStock")]
[HttpPost]
public IActionResult AddStock(string stockId)
{
    var stockModel = new StockModel();
    stockModel.StockId = stockId;
    try
    {
        stockDbEntities = new StockDbContext();
        StockMaster stockMaster = new StockMaster();
        stockMaster.StockId = stockModel.StockId;
        stockMaster.StockName = stockModel.StockName;
        stockMaster.BuyPrice = stockModel.BuyPrice;
        stockMaster.Qty = stockModel.Qty;
        stockMaster.IsActive = stockModel.IsActive;
        stockDbEntities.StockMasters.Add(stockMaster);
        stockDbEntities.SaveChanges();
    }
```

```csharp
            catch (Exception ex)
            {
                return NotFound();
            }
            return Ok(true);
        }

        [HttpGet]
        public List<StockMaster> GetActiveStock()
        {
            stockDbEntities = new StockDbContext();
            var stockmasters = stockDbEntities.StockMasters.Where(x =>
            x.IsActive == true).ToList();
            return stockmasters;
        }

        [Route("~/api/GetStockData/{ticker}/{start}/{end}/{period}")]
        [HttpGet]
public async Task<List<StockModel>> GetStockData(string ticker = "",
string start = "", string end = "", string period = "")
        {
            var p = AlphaVantage.Net.Common.Intervals.Interval.Monthly;
            var stockClosingData = GetStocksDataByDate(ticker, Convert.
            ToDateTime(start), Convert.ToDateTime(end), period).Result;
            List<StockModel> models = new List<StockModel>();
            foreach (var r in stockClosingData)
            {
                models.Add(new StockModel
                {
                    StockId = ticker,
                    StockName = ticker,
                    Date = r.Time.ToString("yyyy-MM-dd"),
                    Open = r.OpeningPrice,
                    High = r.HighestPrice,
                    Low = r.LowestPrice,
```

```
                Close = r.ClosingPrice,
                Volume = r.Volume
            });
        }
        return models.ToList();
    }

    private async Task<IEnumerable<StockDataPoint>>
    GetStocksDataByDate(string stockId, DateTime startDate, DateTime
    endDate, string period = "")
    {
        StockTimeSeries stockTs = null;
        string apiKey = "2";
        using var client = new AlphaVantageClient(apiKey);
        using var stocksClient = client.Stocks();
        if ((period == "daily") || (period.IsNullOrEmpty()))
        {
            stockTs = await stocksClient.GetTimeSeriesAsync(stockId,
            Interval.Daily, OutputSize.Compact, isAdjusted: true);
        }
        else if (period == "monthly")
        {
stockTs = await stocksClient.GetTimeSeriesAsync(stockId, Interval.Monthly,
OutputSize.Compact, isAdjusted: true);
        }

        var query = stockTs.DataPoints.Where(c => c.Time >= startDate
        && c.Time <= endDate);
        return query.ToList();
    }

    [Route("~/api/GetGainerLoserStockData/{ticker}/{period}")]
    [HttpGet]
    public async Task<List<StockModel>> GetGainerLoserStockData(string
    ticker = "", string period = "")
    {
        var p = AlphaVantage.Net.Common.Intervals.Interval.Monthly;
```

```
var startDate = DateTime.Now.AddMonths(-11);
var endDate = DateTime.Now;
var stockClosingData = GetStocksDataByDate(ticker, startDate,
endDate).Result;
List<StockModel> models = new List<StockModel>();
foreach (var r in stockClosingData)
{
    models.Add(new StockModel
    {
        StockId = ticker,
        StockName = ticker,
        Date = r.Time.ToString("yyyy-MM-dd"),
        Open = r.OpeningPrice,
        High = r.HighestPrice,
        Low = r.LowestPrice,
        Close = r.ClosingPrice,
        Volume = r.Volume
    });
}
return models.ToList();
        }
    }
}
```

Press F5 and run the code. Your web API will start running. See Figure 7-13. Now let's develop an Angular app using Highcharts. If you want to learn how to configure the new Angular app, please refer to Chapter 3.

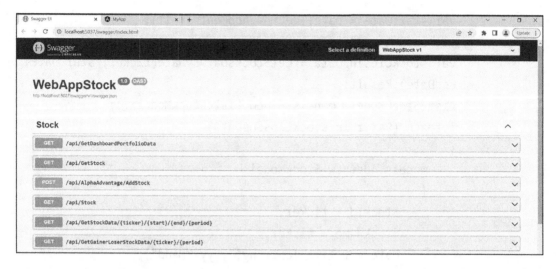

Figure 7-13. *Swagger Swashbuckle API*

Routing in an Angular App

For navigation between different pages, routing plays an essential role. Every application has different pages, and routing is a way for the user to communicate between different pages. Figure 7-14 describes the application architecture. For this application, you have index.html, which calls appComponent. In this part, all menus are configured; when a user clicks a menu, that respective component is called.

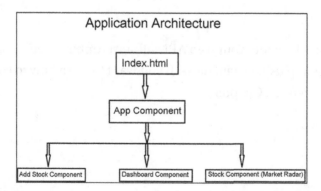

Figure 7-14. *Application architecture for the e-portfolio learning app*

If you want to configure routing in your application, first you must import RouterModule from '@angular/router' into the app.module.ts file and then, with the use of .forRoot([ ]), define the path and component properties.

- path: Here you can define the URL. For example, when a user clicks the dashboard, it will redirect to the localhost/dashboard. Whatever name you specify in the path area must be the same name defined in an anchor tag in the HTML page. The next example will explain this in more detail.

- component: In this property, you define the name of the component you want to call at the time of the menu click.

Example:

```
import {RouterModule} from '@angular/router'
imports: [
RouterModule.forRoot([
{ path: 'stock', component: StockComponent },
{ path: 'dashboard', component: DashboardComponent },
    ])
]
```

In the above example, in the .forRoot method array, you define path and component for all three menus. Now copy Listing 7-5's code into the app.module.ts file so you can enable routing in your application.

Listing 7-5. app.module.ts

```
import { NgModule } from '@angular/core';
import { BrowserModule } from '@angular/platform-browser';
import { AppRoutingModule } from './app-routing.module';
import { AppComponent } from './app.component';
import { HttpClientModule } from '@angular/common/http';
import { AddstockComponent } from './addstock/addstock.component';
import { DashboardComponent } from './dashboard/dashboard.component';
import { RouterModule } from '@angular/router'
import { FormsModule, ReactiveFormsModule } from '@angular/forms';
import { StockComponent } from './stock/stock.component';
```

```
@NgModule({
  declarations: [
    AppComponent,
    AddstockComponent,
    DashboardComponent,
    StockComponent
  ],
  imports: [
    BrowserModule,
    AppRoutingModule,
    HighchartsChartModule,
    HttpClientModule,
    FormsModule,
    ReactiveFormsModule,
    RouterModule.forRoot([
      { path: 'stock', component: StockComponent },
      { path: 'dashboard', component: DashboardComponent },
    ])
  ],
  providers: [],
  bootstrap: [AppComponent]
})
export class AppModule { }
```

Now open app.component.ts and add Listing 7-6's code.

Listing 7-6. app.component.ts

```
import { Component } from '@angular/core';
@Component({
selector: 'app-root',
templateUrl: './app.component.html',
styleUrls: ['./app.component.css']
})
export class AppComponent {
constructor() {
  }
```

```
ngOnInit() {
  }
}
```

In this file, nothing is special because app.component.ts only provides the HTML and CSS; when the user clicks the hyperlinks, it will redirect to a different component. Now copy Listing 7-7's code into app.component.css.

Listing 7-7. app.component.css

```
.topnav {
background-color: #333;
overflow: hidden;
  }
    /* Style the links inside the navigation bar */
  .topnav a {
float: left;
color: #f2f2f2;
text-align: center;
padding: 14px 16px;
text-decoration: none;
font-size: 17px;
  }
    /* Change the color of links on hover */
  .topnav a:hover {
background-color: #ddd;
color: black;
  }
    /* Add a color to the active/current link */
  .topnava.active {
background-color: rgb(221, 97, 25);
color: white;
  }
```

Open app.component.html and copy Listing 7-8's code. Here you configure your menu hyperlinks.

Listing 7-8. app.component.html

```
<div class="topnav">
<a class="active" [routerLink]="['/dashboard']">Dashboard</a>
<a [routerLink]="['/stock']">Market Radar</a>
</div>
<br/>
<router-outlet></router-outlet>
```

In Listing 7-8, the [routerLink] directive is used to open your routing path at the time of the click. This is directly linked with RouterModule.forEach([]), which you define in app.module.ts.

Now it's time to add a model class for your Angular application. The class name is stockmodel.ts, so open a new terminal window in Visual Studio and type the following command and press Enter. This command will add a stockmodel.ts file into the model folder.

```
ng generate class model/stockmodel
```

Now copy Listing 7-9's code into the stockmodel.ts file.

Listing 7-9. stockmodel.ts

```
export class Stockmodel
{
    public stockName: string = "";
    public date: string  = "";
    public Open: number = 0;
    public high: number = 0;
    public Low: number = 0;
    public Close: number = 0;
    public Volume: number = 0;
    public stockId:string = "";
    public BuyPrice:number = 0;
    public Qty: number = 0;
    public IsActive:boolean = false;
    public TotalInvested:number = 0;
```

```
    public CurrentValue:number = 0;
    public TotalGain:number = 0;
}
```

You can see that this model class property is the same as you created in the web
API model class. The reason to create this file is so that whenever you send the request
to the web API, you will receive data into Stockmodel at the time of response. After the
response, this model will also help generate data binding into different charts.

Now it's time to add a service to your Angular application. In this application, you
have only one service file, which will communicate with the web API to insert and fetch
records based on the requirements. To create a service file, type the following command
into the terminal window of Visual Studio. This command will create a stock.service.ts
file in the services folder.

```
ng generate service services/stock
```

Now, copy Listing 7-10's code into the stock.service.ts file.

Listing 7-10. stock.service.ts

```typescript
import { Injectable } from '@angular/core';
import { HttpClient } from '@angular/common/http';
import { Stockmodel } from '../model/stockmodel';
import { Observable } from 'rxjs';
import { tick } from '@angular/core/testing';

@Injectable({
  providedIn: 'root'
})
export class StockService {
  constructor(private http: HttpClient) {
    console.log('Stock Service called');
  }

  GetStockByTicks(url:string, ticker: string, start: string, end: string,
  period: string): Observable<Stockmodel[]> {

    return this.http.get<Stockmodel[]>(url + "/" + ticker + "/" + start +
    "/" + end + "/" + period);
  }
```

```
GetGainerLoserStockData(url:string, ticker: string, period: string):
Observable<Stockmodel[]> {

    return this.http.get<Stockmodel[]>(url + "/" + ticker + "/" + period);
}

GetStocks(url:string): Observable<Stockmodel[]> {

    return this.http.get<Stockmodel[]>(url);
  }
}
```

If you want to learn more about httpClient, Observable, and providerIn, please refer to Chapter 5, where I describe how to communicate with the Angular service in more detail.

Now one by one you will add new components and connect them with stock. service.ts.

Here you must remember one thing: once you run your web API application, you will get a port like (:5037) or any other port number, like https://localhost:5037/. Whatever port number you get for your web API, use the same port in the URL variable in the component.ts file; otherwise, the request will never go to the web API. Follow this practice for all upcoming components.

Now it's time to add stock.component.ts, where you define your market radar and where users can search for stock performance daily and monthly based on selected dates. Type the following command into the terminal window of Visual Studio:

```
ng generate component stock
```

This command will add the stock.component.ts file into your folder structure.

Now copy Listing 7-11's code into the stock.component.ts file.

Listing 7-11. stock.component.ts

```
import { Component, OnInit } from '@angular/core';
import { Stockmodel } from '../model/stockmodel';
import { StockService } from '../services/stock.service';
import { FormBuilder, FormGroup, Validators, FormControl,FormArray } from
"@angular/forms";
```

```
import * as Highcharts from 'highcharts';

@Component({
  selector: 'app-stock',
  templateUrl: './stock.component.html',
  styleUrls: ['./stock.component.css']
})

export class StockComponent implements OnInit {
  url: string = 'http://localhost:5037/api/GetStockData';
  addForm: FormGroup = new FormGroup({});
  start: any;
  end: any = "";
  stockDates: any;
  stockModel: Stockmodel[] = [];
  SelStockId: any;
  SelPeriodId: any;
  Stocks: any[] = [];

  constructor(private stockService: StockService, private formBuilder:
  FormBuilder) {
  }
  public options: any = {
    chart: {
      type: 'line',
    },
    title: {
      text: 'E- Portfolio'
    },
    credits: {
      enabled: false
    },
    xAxis: {
      categories: [],
    },
```

```
    yAxis: {
      title: {
        text: ''
      },
    },
    series: [],
  }
ngOnInit() {
    this.StockDDL();
    this.addForm = this.formBuilder.group({
      Stock: ['', Validators.required],
      Period: ['', Validators.required],
      StartDate: ['', Validators.required],
      EndDate: ['', Validators.required],
    });
}
onSubmit() {
    this.SelStockId = this.addForm.get('Stock');
    this.start = this.addForm.get('StartDate');
    this.end = this.addForm.get('EndDate');
    this.SelPeriodId = this.addForm.get('Period');
    this.stockService.GetStockByTicks(this.url, this.SelStockId.value,
    this.start.value, this.end.value, this.SelPeriodId.value)
      .toPromise().then(data => {
        const stockData:any = [];
        const dates:any = [];
        if (data != null)
        {
          for (let i = 0; i < data.length; i++) {
            const temp_row = [
              data[i].high,
            ];
            dates.push(data[i].date);
            stockData.push(data[i].high);
          }
        }
```

```
      this.stockModel = stockData;
      this.stockDates = dates;
      var dataSeries = [];
      for (var i = 0; i < this.stockModel.length; i++) {
        dataSeries.push(
          this.stockModel[i]
        );
      }
      this.options.series = [{ data: dataSeries, name: this.SelStockId.
      value }]
      this.options.xAxis.categories = this.stockDates
      Highcharts.chart('container', this.options);
    },
      error => {
        console.log('Something went wrong.');
      });
  }
StockDDL() {
      this.stockService.GetStocks("http://localhost:5037/api/getstock")
    .toPromise().then(data => {
      const stockLData:any = [];
      if(data!=null)
      {
        for(let i=0; i<data.length;i++)
        {
          stockLData.push({
            StockName: data[i].stockName,
            StockId: data[i].stockId
          });
        }
      }

      return this.Stocks = stockLData;
    });
  }
}
```

In Listing 7-11, you have three methods. The first is StockDDL(), which is responsible for fetching data from the StockMaster table and binding it in the dropdown list; this method calls the ngOnInit() method. As you already know, the ngOninit() method runs automatically at the time of page load, so whenever this page loads the first time, this will bind active stock information into the dropdown list.

Next is the onSubmit() method. This method generates an event once the user clicks the Search button. This method sends all field parameters to the GetstockByTicks() service method. At the time of response, it collects information from the Alpha Vantage API service based on data that will populate the line charts using Highcharts. If you want to learn this process in more detail, please refer to Chapter 5.

Now copy Listing 7-12's code into the stock.component.html file.

Listing 7-12. stock.component.html

```
<form [formGroup]="addForm" novalidate class="form"
(ngSubmit)="onSubmit()">
    <div>
        <hr/>
      <table>
        <tr>
          <td>
            Select Stock*
          </td>
          <td>
 <select  class="form-control" formControlName="Stock">
 <option *ngFor="let Stock of Stocks" value={{Stock.StockId}}>
                    {{Stock.StockName}}
                </option>
            </select>
          </td>
          <td>
            Period*
          </td>
          <td>
  <select  class="form-control"  formControlName="Period" >
                <option selected value="daily">Daily</option>
```

```
            <option value="monthly">Monthly</option>
          </select>
        </td>
        <td>
          Start Date*
        </td>
        <td>
<input type="date" id="txtStartDate"

formControlName="StartDate"/>
        </td>
        <td>
          End Date*
        </td>
        <td>
   <input type="date" id="txtEndDate" formControlName="EndDate"/>
        </td>
        <td>
          <button type='submit'>Search</button>
        </td>
      </tr>
    </table>
    <hr/>
  </div>

  <div class="content" id="container" role="main">
  </div>
  </form>
  <router-outlet></router-outlet>
```

In the Listing 7-12 code, your chart will populate the container <div> once the user clicks the Search button.

After adding the stock and market radar features, you can start the development of the dashboard feature. Type the following command into the terminal window of Visual Studio:

```
ng generate component dashboard
```

In the `dashboard.component.ts` code, there are three sections. In the top section, you get all the stocks tables you added into the `StockMaster` table. After that is a button called Dashboard Chart. When you click this button, you will get three charts in the dashboard.

1. **Profit/Loss chart**: This is a pie chart that tells you about the profit/loss of the portfolio.

2. **Top Gainer Stock chart**: This is a line chart. It finds and shows the most profitable stock from your portfolio and its performance.

3. **Top Loser Stock chart**: This is a line chart; it finds the worst performing stock from your portfolio and displays its performance.

Now copy Listing 7-13's code into the `dashboard.component.ts` file.

Listing 7-13. dashboard.component.ts

```
import { Component, OnInit } from '@angular/core';
import { Stockmodel } from '../model/stockmodel';
import { StockService } from '../services/stock.service';
import { FormBuilder, FormGroup, Validators } from "@angular/forms";
import * as Highcharts from 'highcharts';

@Component({
  selector: 'app-dashboard',
  templateUrl: './dashboard.component.html',
  styleUrls: ['./dashboard.component.css']
})
export class DashboardComponent implements OnInit {
  addForm: FormGroup = new FormGroup({});
  url: string = 'http://localhost:5037/api/GetStockData';
  Stocks: Stockmodel[] = [];
  PortfolioStocks: any;//For holding Portfolio data with profit/loss.
  constructor(private stockService: StockService, private formBuilder:
  FormBuilder) {
  }
```

```
ngOnInit() {
   // this.GetActiveStocks();
   this.GetDashboardPortfolioData();
}
GetDashboardPortfolioData() {
   this.stockService.GetStocks("http://localhost:5037/api/
   GetDashboardPortfolioData")
     .toPromise().then(data => {

       return this.PortfolioStocks = data;
     });
}
public profitLossChart: any = {
   chart: {
     type: 'pie',
   },
   title: {
     text: 'Profit/Loss Chart'
   },
   credits: {
     enabled: false
   },
   series: [],
}
GetProfitLossChart() {
   let totalInvestment: number = 0;
   let totalGain: number = 0;
   for(let i=0; i< this.PortfolioStocks.length;i++)
   {
     totalInvestment += this.PortfolioStocks[i].totalInvested;
     totalGain += this.PortfolioStocks[i].currentValue;
   }

   this.GetTopGainerChart();
   this.GetTopLoserChart();
```

```
    this.profitLossChart.series = [{
      data: [{
        name: 'Total Investment#',
        y: totalInvestment,
      },
      {
        name: 'Current Value',
        y: totalGain,
      }]
    }]
    Highcharts.chart('containerProfitLoss', this.profitLossChart);
  }
  public topGainerChart: any = {
    chart: {
      type: 'line',
    },
    title: {
      text: 'Top Gainer'
    },
    credits: {
      enabled: false
    },
    xAxis: {
      categories: [],
    },
    yAxis: {
      title: {
        text: ''
      },
    },
    series: [],
  }
  GetTopGainerChart() {
    let length = this.PortfolioStocks.length;
    if (length > 0) {
```

```
  this.stockService.GetGainerLoserStockData('http://localhost:5037/
  api/GetGainerLoserStockData', this.PortfolioStocks[length - 1].
  stockId, "Monthly")
    .toPromise().then(data => {

      const stockData:any = [];
      const dates:any = [];
      if(data!=null)
      {
        for(let i = 0; i<data.length; i++)
        {

          const temp_row = [
            data[i].high,
          ];
          dates.push(data[i].date);
          stockData.push(data[i].high);

        }
      }

      var dataSeries = [];
      for (var i = 0; i < stockData.length; i++) {
        dataSeries.push(
          stockData[i]
        );
      }
      this.topGainerChart.series = [{ data: dataSeries, name: this.
      PortfolioStocks[length - 1].stockId }]
      this.topGainerChart.xAxis.categories = dates
  Highcharts.chart('topGainerChart', this.topGainerChart);
    },
      error => {
        console.log('Something went wrong.');
      });
  }
}
```

```
public topLoserChart: any = {
  chart: {
    type: 'line',
  },
  title: {
    text: 'Top Loser'
  },
  credits: {
    enabled: false
  },
  xAxis: {
    categories: [],
  },
  yAxis: {
    title: {
      text: ''
    },
  },
  series: [],
}
GetTopLoserChart() {
  let length = this.PortfolioStocks.length;
  if (length > 0) {
    this.stockService.GetGainerLoserStockData('http://localhost:5037/
    api/GetGainerLoserStockData', this.PortfolioStocks[0].stockId,
    "Monthly")
      .toPromise().then(data => {
        const stockData:any = [];
        const dates:any = [];
        if(data!=null)
        {
          for(var i=0; i<data.length;i++)
          {
            const temp_row = [
              data[i].high,
            ];
```

```
        dates.push(data[i].date);
        stockData.push(data[i].high);
      }
    }

    var dataSeries = [];
    for (var i = 0; i < stockData.length; i++) {
      dataSeries.push(
        stockData[i]
      );
    }
    this.topLoserChart.series = [{ data: dataSeries, name: this.
    PortfolioStocks[0].stockId }]
    this.topLoserChart.xAxis.categories = dates
    Highcharts.chart('topLoserChart', this.topLoserChart);
  },
    error => {

      console.log('Something went wrong.');
    });
  }
  }
}
```

In Listing 7-13, there are five methods. Let's explore each one.

1. GetDashboardPortfolioData(): This method populates data
    into a grid. After getting a response from the service, it stores
    data into the this.portfolioStocks variable. This variable is a
    stockmodel[] array type variable.

2. ngOnInit(): Here you call the GetDashboardPortfolioData()
    method. The idea is that once page load, this will show a grid.

3. GetTopGainerChart(): This method sends the request to the
    GetGainerLoserStockData() service method, and at the time of
    return, generates a data series for a line chart.

4. GetTopLoserChart(): This method sends the request to the
    GetGainerLoserStockData() service method. At the time of
    response, it generates a data series for a line chart for the worst
    performing stock into the portfolio.

5. GetProfitLossChart(): This method binds a data series for the
    pie chart. This is reflected in the dashboard after a dashboard
    button click. Internally it calls the GetTopGainerChart() and
    GetTopLoserChart() methods.

Now copy Listing 7-14's code into dashboard.component.html.

Listing 7-14. dashboard.component.html

```
<table border="1" style="border-color: black; border-collapse: collapse;
margin-left: 35%">
    <thead>
      <tr>
        <th>StockId</th>
        <th>Stock Name</th>
        <th>Buy Price</th>
        <th>Qty</th>
        <th>TotalInvested</th>
        <th>CurrentValue</th>
        <th>TotalGain</th>
      </tr>
    </thead>
    <tbody>
      <tr *ngFor="let stock of PortfolioStocks">
        <td class="hidden">{{stock.stockId}}</td>
        <td>{{stock.stockName}}</td>
        <td>{{stock.buyPrice}}</td>
        <td>{{stock.qty}}</td>
        <td>{{stock.totalInvested}}</td>
        <td>{{stock.currentValue}}</td>
        <td>{{stock.totalGain}}</td>
      </tr>
```

```
    </tbody>
  </table>
<div>
    <input style="margin-left: 45%; margin-bottom: 10px;" type="button"
    id="btnProfitLoss" value="Dashboard Chart"
        (click)="GetProfitLossChart()"/>
</div>
<table border="1" style="width: 100%; color: black; border-color: black;
border-collapse: collapse;">
  <tr>
        <td style="width: 50%">
<div class="containerProfitLoss" id="containerProfitLoss" role="main">
          </div>
    </td>
    <td>
 <div class="topGainerChart" id="topGainerChart" role="main">
          </div>
    </td>
  </tr>
  <tr>
      <td>
      </td>
      <td>
   <div class="topLoserChart" id="topLoserChart" role="main">
          </div>
      </td>
    </tr>
</table>
```

Your application is ready to take off. First, run your web API application and then come to the Angular app and type ng serve in the terminal window of Visual Studio and press Enter. You will get the output shown in Figure 7-15.

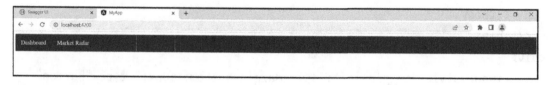

Figure 7-15. *Home page with menus*

Click the Market Radar menu. You will get the output shown in Figure 7-16.

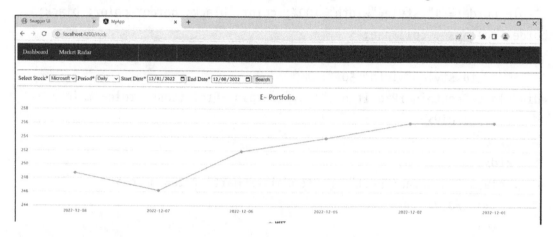

Figure 7-16. *Market radar for selected stock*

Now it's time to see the dashboard. On the panel is one table grid, one pie chart, and two line charts (Figure 7-17).

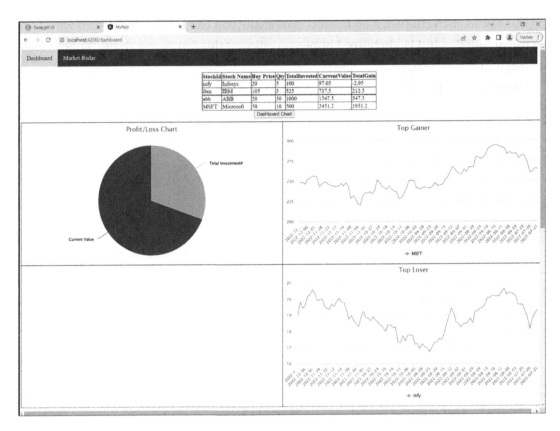

Figure 7-17. *Dashboard screen*

You saw how easily you can develop a complete application and build an interactive dashboard using Angular and Highcharts with a web API.

Summary

In this chapter, you developed an e-portfolio learning application with the use of a web API, Angular, and Highcharts. You also learned how to create routing and forms modules so your controls can communicate with components to service a user very efficiently. You also learn how to consume the Alpha Vantage Finance API from the NuGet package so you can get historical stock data. With the use of Angular and Highcharts, you can develop your charts more interactively and quickly.

You saw in each chapter, step by step, how easily you can build a dashboard with the use of Angular and Highcharts. I hope you enjoyed this journey with me. Thanks for reading and for your support.

Happy programming!

Index

© Sourabh Mishra 2023
S. Mishra, *Practical Highcharts with Angular*, https://doi.org/10.1007/978-1-4842-9181-8

I, J, K

L

T, U

V

W, X, Y

Z

Printed in the United States
by Baker & Taylor Publisher Services